WAITING FOR CHRISTMAS

WEEKLY FAMILY DEVOTIONALS FOR ADVENT

BY NANCY RUTH

Parent Road Ministries materials may be ordered by contacting:

Parent Road Ministries
P.O. Box 397
Tonkawa, OK 74653
www.ParentRoadMin.com
239-462-4686

Because of the dynamic nature of the Internet, any web addresses or links contained in this book may have changed since publication and may no longer be valid.

Paperback ISBN # 1-970061-00-6
E-book ISBN # 1-970061-01-4

Printed in the United States of America

Contents

Before You Start

There are a few things you need to know before you begin this family devotional. First the legal stuff.

This book is copyrighted. If you give a copy to a friend without paying for it, that is ***stealing***.

The FREE *Waiting for Christmas: Advent Readings for Corporate Worship* and the complete *Waiting for Christmas: Weekly Family Devotionals for Advent* are available online at http://parentroadmin.com/store-4/.

Email us at info@parentroadmin.com to discuss bulk pricing.

1. Who is this for?

This devotional is designed for families to do together. Each lesson comes in three different levels so you can choose what best fits your family.

- **Preschool** lessons are designed for toddlers through four year olds (Pre-K). If you have mostly little children with the oldest under seven, we recommend doing this lesson as a family.

- **Children** lessons are designed for ages six through nine. If you have mostly younger children with the oldest under thirteen, we recommend doing this lesson as a family.

- **Preteen** lessons are designed for ages ten through thirteen. If you have mostly preteens and teenagers, we recommend doing this lesson as a family.

Do you have a wide span of ages in your home?

Why not do a younger lesson together as a family, dismiss the younger children to play, and then do an older lesson with those children? That way the family does it together and everyone can get something out of it.

2. How does this work?

Each lesson is available on three levels: Preschool, Children, or Youth (see explanation above). Lessons include the same main point, but different levels of study based on the age.

Each lesson includes:

- **Advent Candle Guide** (optional) – which candles to light
- **Opening Prayer**
- **Bible Reading** – You will need your own Bible. If you don't have one, try http://www.biblegateway.com. They also have an app.
- **Devotional**
- **Song Suggestions**
- **Family Fun** – a learning or application activity to do together

3. When should we start?

Advent is the name of the four weeks before Christmas. It usually begins the last Sunday in November (immediately after Thanksgiving in the United States).

Is it already December? Don't worry. Just start this week and keep going. The message of Christmas is important year-round, not just during the month of December.

During Advent, Christians around the world remember how special Jesus is as they look forward to celebrating His birth.

Did you know Jesus wasn't actually born on Christmas Day?

No one knows for sure the actual date of Jesus' birth, though speculation began as early as Polycarp (c.69-c.155). One of the earliest church celebrations was Epiphany on January 6, the date the magi arrived with gifts for the Christ child. December 25 was chosen to celebrate His birth in about AD 273 because of two pagan Roman festivals celebrated on that day. The idea was that Jesus was the Son of God, so His birth should be celebrated instead of the birth of the sun in the sky.

Emperor Constantine solidified the date of this celebration in 336 when he declared Christianity to be official religion of the Roman Empire. Some Eastern Orthodox churches celebrate Christmas 13 days later because of the Gregorian Calendar which was not adopted by everyone.[1]

4. How to Set Up a Family Advent Wreath (optional)

You can celebrate Advent at home by lighting a candle (or turning on a battery-operated candle) and reading this short devotional together once a week. This is **OPTIONAL**, but it adds a bit of festivity to your family devotions.

Here's how it works. Each week, one more candle is lit during Advent Readings. Candles may also be lit other times, like for meals. The white center candle is always last, and is saved for Christmas Eve and Christmas Day.

---

[1] For more information, see Elesha Coffman, "Why December 25?" Christian History.net (Christianity Today, 8 August 2008); Internet, accessed 30 August 2014.

All you need to make your wreath are four or five candles and, if you would like, some evergreen. Not all wreaths use the fifth candle in the center, but that's my favorite one.

Usually, four of the candles are arraigned in a circle of evergreen with a fifth white candle in the middle. A few more creative Advent Wreaths, however, have used floating candles, or arraigned the five pillar candles in a row with the white candle in the center.

These candles may be any shape or size. Sometimes the center candle is thicker than the others. Some traditions have four blue candles, some all purple, and some have one pink (rose) and three purple. Please note that if mixed colors are used, the pink candle is added the third week.

Half the fun is setting up your wreath. In my Sunday school class we make one each year on the bulletin board stapling green handprints, red berries, and paper candles (similar to Figure 8 below, but flat on the wall). Each week I add a little yellow tissue paper "flame" to the new candle. How will your family do theirs?

Below are some pictures of advent wreaths I found online with the web links where I found them. I accessed these sites on October 14, 2017. They may or may not still be valid when you click them. Unfortunately, that's the internet for you!

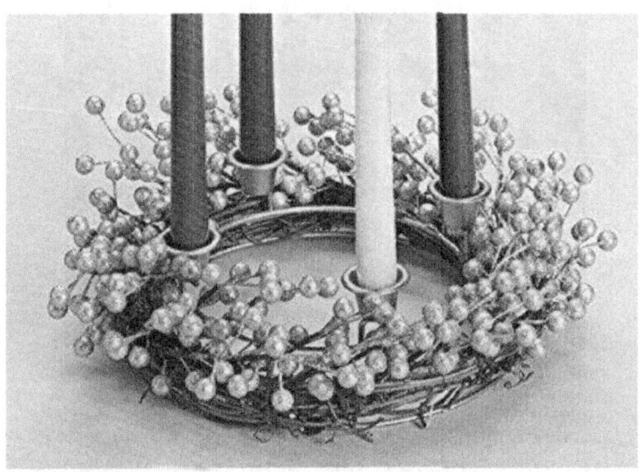

Figure 1: Champagne Berry Christmas Advent Wreath from
https://www.amazon.com/dp/B00V3LWPVM/ref=asc_df_B00V3LWPVM5215924/?tag=hyprod-20&creative=395033&creativeASIN=B00V3LWPVM&linkCode=df0&hvadid=191967931333&hvpos=1o5&hvnetw=g&hvrand=10308102389652123065&hvpone=&hvptwo=&hvqmt=&hvdev=c&hvdvcmdl=&hvlocint=&hvlocphy=9026683&hvtargid=pla-300508336542

Figure 2: DIY Advent Wreath by
http://becomingpeculiar.com/my-eco-friendly-diy-advent-wreath/

Figure 4: Painted Votive Advent Wreath by
http://www.whitehouseblackshutters.com/painted-votive-advent-wreath/

Figure 3: Children's Advent Wreath from
https://www.stjudeshop.com/shop-seasonal/advent-christmas/advent-candles-wreaths/childrens-advent-wreath/?utm_medium=googleshopping&utm_source=bc&gclid=CjwKCAjw64bPBRApEiwAJhG-fp5dmtSEzvO7ksKiYhZeFoDweFxXN8yuPjMGZbfn_akx2Zhqmv1xIRoCkoIQAvD_BwE

Figure 5: Homemade Advent Wreath by
https://nurturestore.co.uk/homemade-advent-wreath

Figure 8: Advent Paper Hand Wreath from
http://www.alannageorge.com/2008/12/01/advent-activities-advent-paper-hand-wreath/

Figure 6: Make an Advent Wreath from ornaments by
https://deavita.com/dekoration/weihnachtsdeko-ideen/adventskranz-kugeln-selber-machen-anleitung-ideen.html

Figure 7: Advent Wreath from the Kitchen from
http://smallnotebook.org/2009/11/28/advent-wreath-from-the-kitchen/

Now that you're all set, we've got one more item of business before we get started.

5. Which Candle to Light When (optional)

An advent wreath is made up of either 4 blue, 4 purple, or 1 pink and 3 purple candles (see page 3 above). The four candles are placed evenly in an evergreen wreath surrounding one white candle.

Each week, light the previous weeks' candles before moving on to the new one. You may also choose to have the previous weeks' candles already lit and simply light the new one. Once lit, the appropriate candles should burn for the rest of your devotional time. Candles may also be lit at meals or other times.

The order (going clockwise) should be: Hope (week 1, purple if using a multi-colored set), Preparation (week 2, purple if using a multi-colored set), Joy (week 3, pink if using a multi-colored set), Love (week 4, purple if using a multi-colored set), and the Christ candle (Christmas Eve and/or Christmas Day, white if using a multi-colored set).

Preschool Lessons

PRESCHOOL WEEK 1: HOPE

GOD ALWAYS KEEPS HIS PROMISES

Today's Bible Verses

It may be helpful to look up these verses and bookmark them in advance. Older children and teens can help you.

Don't have a Bible at home? Try http://biblegateway.com. Type the reference below, hit enter, and it will take you right to it.

- Numbers 23:19

- Isaiah 35:5 (included in the text below)

- Matthew 9:27-31 (summarized below)

- Mark 7:31-37 (summarized below)

Advent Wreath Candle Guide

Each week, light the previous weeks' candles before moving on to the new one. You may also choose to have the previous weeks' candles already lit and simply light the new one. Once lit, the appropriate candles should burn for the rest of your devotional time. Candles may also be lit at meals or other times.

Today we start with the candle of Hope (purple if using a multi-colored set).

Opening Prayer

Dear God, thank You that You always keep Your promises. Please help us to trust You. Amen.

Do you know what a promise is? (Allow children to answer if they think they know.) A promise is when you tell someone you will do something.

Have you ever made a promise? Tell me about what happened.

Sometimes people keep their promises and sometimes they don't. God always keeps His promises. When you hear me say "God always keeps His promises," I want you to say it back to me. Let's practice. Are you ready? (normal voice) God always keeps His promises. "God always keeps His promises." Let's say that really loud. Remember that I go first. Ready? (loudly) GOD ALWAYS KEEPS HIS PROMISES! "GOD ALWAYS KEEPS HIS PROMISES!" Good.

Now let's see how quietly we can say it. Ready? (whisper) God always keeps His promises. "God always keeps His promises." Very good.

Here is a promise I make you. I promise that we are going to read the Bible. Are you ready?

Bible Reading

Numbers is a book in the Bible. Chapter 23, verse 19 says:

"God isn't a mere human. He can't lie.
He isn't a human being. He doesn't change his mind.
He speaks, and then he acts.
He makes a promise, and then he keeps it" (NIRV).

(whisper) God always keeps His promises. "God always keeps His promises."

Let's see some of the promises that God made.

A long time before Jesus was born,[2] God gave a man named Isaiah a promise about what Jesus would do. We can read that promise in Isaiah 35:5. As we read this verse, let's act it out. Ready?

God said, "Then the eyes of those who are blind will be opened" (NIRV). Put your hands over your eyes. (Do it with them so they can see what you mean.) Now open your eyes and see!

God said, "The ears of those who can't hear will be unplugged" (NIRV). Cover your ears. (Do it with them so they can see what you mean.) Now open your ears and hear!

(whisper) God always keeps His promises. "God always keeps His promises."

––––––––––––––––––––––––––––––

[2] More precisely, Isaiah's prophetic ministry lasted from 742 B.C. to at least 701 B.C. Jesus was born in either 6 or 4 B.C. See Thomas Brisco, *Holman Bible Atlas* (Nashville: Broadman & Holman Publishers, 1998), 141, 217.

That was fun! Let's see if Jesus did those things. Are you ready?

Matthew 9:27-31 tells us about two blind men who asked Jesus to heal them. What do you think Jesus did? (Let children answer.) Jesus touched their eyes and healed them! Put your hands over your eyes. (Do it with them so they can see what you mean.) Now open your eyes and see!

Did God keep His promise that Jesus would help blind people see? (Let children answer.)

(normal voice) God always keeps His promises. "God always keeps His promises."

Let's remember God's promises in Isaiah 35:5. Ready?

God said, "Then the eyes of those who are blind will be opened" (NIRV). Put your hands over your eyes. (Do it with them so they can see what you mean.) Now open your eyes and see!

God said, "The ears of those who can't hear will be unplugged" (NIRV). Cover your ears. (Do it with them so they can see what you mean.) Now open your ears and hear!

God kept His promise that Jesus would heal blind people. Let's see if He healed deaf people too.

Mark 7:31-37 tells about some people who brought a deaf man to Jesus. This man couldn't hear and couldn't talk. They asked Jesus to heal their friend. Jesus prayed and touched him. Then the man could hear and talk! Cover your ears. (Do it with them so they can see what you mean.) Now open your ears and hear!

Did God keep His promise that Jesus would help deaf people hear? (Let children answer.) Did God keep His promise that Jesus would help blind people see? (Let children answer.)

(loudly) GOD ALWAYS KEEPS HIS PROMISES! "GOD ALWAYS KEEPS HIS PROMISES!" Yes, He does.

Suggested Songs
The songs below are considered by some to be standard children's songs. As such, they should be easily available in online videos and audio tracks.

- "We Three Kings" (The kings trusted God's promise that Jesus would be born.)

- "Jingle Bells" (At Christmas we celebrate Jesus' birthday. God promised Jesus would come. God always keeps His promises.)

Family Fun

Let's see what it might have been like to be blind.

SUPPLIES NEEDED:

- Blindfold or some kind of visual screen (see below)

- Items of different textures

Take turns touching items of different textures (without a blindfold).

What do you feel?

Is it round or does it have corners?

Is it hard or soft?

 Is it smooth or rough?

Now try touching the same items again, this time without looking. Use a blindfold if you like or gently cover children's eyes. You may also put a piece of paper or other visual screen between the children and the item so they cannot see what they are touching.

What do you feel?

Is it round or does it have corners?

Is it hard or soft?

Is it smooth or rough?

Can you tell what you are touching? What is it?

Some people wear glasses to help them see. Jesus didn't need glasses. Jesus healed a blind man so he could see even without glasses!

(whisper) God always keeps His promises. "God always keeps His promises."

PRESCHOOL WEEK 2: PEACE
GOD IS ALWAYS WITH US

Today's Bible Verses

It may be helpful to look up these verses and bookmark them in advance. Older children and teens can help you.

Don't have a Bible at home? Try http://biblegateway.com. Type the reference below, hit enter, and it will take you right to it.

- Isaiah 9:6

- John 14:27

Advent Wreath Candle Guide

Each week, light the previous weeks' candles before moving on to the new one. You may also choose to have the previous weeks' candles already lit and simply light the new one. Once lit, the appropriate candles should burn for the rest of your devotional time. Candles may also be lit at meals or other times.

Today we light two candles: last week's candle of Hope and this week's candle of Peace (both are purple if using a multi-colored set).

Opening Prayer

Dear God, thank You that You are always with us. Help us to have peace knowing You are with us when we're scared. Amen.

Think About It

Do you remember what we talked about last week? (Let children answer.)

(whisper) God always keeps His promises. "God always keeps His promises." Way to go!

One of the things God promises is that He is always with us. Hug yourself and say that with me, "God is always with us." (Say it again together.)

Show me what your face looks like when you're scared. (You do it too.) Now show me what it looks like when you feel safe. (You do it too.)

Peace means that we are quiet and safe. Let's play a quick game to practice. When I say "scared," you pretend to be scared. When I say "peace," you get really quiet and pretend you are safe. Ready? (Play a few rounds.)

Let's see what the Bible says about peace.

Bible Reading

The Bible tells us that Jesus gives us peace. Isaiah 9:6 says:

"For to us a child is born, to us a son is given, and the government will be on his shoulders. And he will be called Wonderful Counselor, Mighty God, Everlasting Father, Prince of Peace" (NIV).

Show me "scared." Show me "peace."

We can have peace because God is always with us. Hug yourself and say that with me, "God is always with us." (Say it again together.)

We celebrate Jesus' birthday at Christmas.[3] When Jesus grew up, He taught His friends about God. Before Jesus died and came back to life again, He told His friends that He would have to go soon. This made Jesus' disciples sad and scared. They did not want Jesus to leave. Show me "scared."

Jesus told His friends not to be scared, but to have peace. Show me "peace."

Jesus said:

"I leave my peace with you. I give my peace to you. I do not give it to you as the world does. Do not let your hearts be troubled. And do not be afraid" (John 14:27 NIRV).

Show me "scared." Show me "peace."

Do you know why we don't have to be afraid? (Let children answer.)

We don't have to be afraid because God is always with us. Hug yourself and say that with me, "God is always with us." (Say it again together.)

Show me "scared." Show me "peace."

Hug yourself and say that with me, "God is always with us." (Say it again together.)

---

[3] See the note about Jesus actual birthday in the introduction to this book.

Suggested Songs

The songs below are considered by some to be standard children's songs. As such, they should be easily available in online videos and audio tracks.

- "My God is so Big"

- "Children Go Where I Send Thee"

- "Standing in the Need of Prayer"

- "Peace Like a River"

- "God is Bigger Than the Boogie Man" (VeggieTales)

Family Fun

Hug yourself and say, "God is always with us." (Say it again together.)

Let's play a game to help us remember that.

This game is much like "Going on a Bear Hunt." Read the rhymes and act out what it describes.

GOD IS ALWAYS WITH ME

(*hug yourself*) God is always with me.

(God is always with me.)

(*shake your head*) I won't be afraid.

(I won't be afraid.)

(*fold hands in prayer*) I will pray to Jesus.

(I will pray to Jesus.)

(*point up*) He will guide my way.

(He will guide my way.)

Uh-oh!

The car!

We're driving in the car.

Even when we're going fast.

Even when we're going slow.

God goes where we go!

(*pretend to drive a car:* Vroom!)

(*hug yourself*) God is always with me.

(God is always with me.)

(*shake your head*) I won't be afraid.

(I won't be afraid.)

(*fold hands in prayer*) I will pray to Jesus.

(I will pray to Jesus.)

(*point up*) He will guide my way.

(He will guide my way.)

Uh-oh!

The swings!

We're playing on the swings.

Even when we're going high.

Even when we're going low.

God goes where we go!

(*pretend to go back and forth on the swings*)

(*hug yourself*) God is always with me.

(God is always with me.)

(*shake your head*) I won't be afraid.

(I won't be afraid.)

(*fold hands in prayer*) I will pray to Jesus.

(I will pray to Jesus.)

(*point up*) He will guide my way.

(He will guide my way.)

Uh-oh!

The lake!

We're swimming in the lake.

Even when we're going fast.

Even when we're going slow.

God goes where we go!

(*pretend to swim*)

(*hug yourself*) God is always with me.

(God is always with me.)

(*shake your head*) I won't be afraid.

(I won't be afraid.)

(*fold hands in prayer*) I will pray to Jesus.

(I will pray to Jesus.)

(*point up*) He will guide my way.

(He will guide my way.)

Uh-oh!

The air!

We're flying in the air.

Even when we're going high.

Even when we're going low.

'Cuz God goes where we go!

(*pretend to fly*)

(*hug yourself*) God is always with me.

(God is always with me.)

(*shake your head*) I won't be afraid.

(I won't be afraid.)

(*fold hands in prayer*) I will pray to Jesus.

(I will pray to Jesus.)

(*point up*) He will guide my way.

(He will guide my way.)

Uh-oh!

The cave!

We're walking in a cave.

Even when we're going high.

Even when we're going low.

God goes where we go!

(*pretend to carefully explore the cave*)

(*hug yourself*) God is always with me.

(God is always with me.)

(*shake your head*) I won't be afraid.

(I won't be afraid.)

(*fold hands in prayer*) I will pray to Jesus.

(I will pray to Jesus.)

(*point up*) He will guide my way.

(He will guide my way.)

Uh-oh!

The roller coaster!

We're riding on the roller coaster.

Even when we're going fast.

Even when we're going slow.

God goes where we go!

(*pretend to go up and down and side to side on a roller coaster*)

Whew!

I'm tired.

Let's go home.

Back through the cave.

(*pretend to carefully explore the cave*)

Back on the airplane.

(*pretend to fly*)

Back through the lake.

(*pretend to swim*)

Back on the swings.

(pretend to go back and forth on the swings)

Back in the car.

(pretend to drive a car: Vroom!)

Oh, good!

We're home.

(hug yourself) God is always with me.

(God is always with me.)

(shake your head) I won't be afraid.

(I won't be afraid.)

(fold hands in prayer) I will pray to Jesus.

(I will pray to Jesus.)

(point up) He will guide my way.

(He will guide my way.)

Before you playing again with older preschoolers, consider reading Psalm 139:7-12 together.

PRESCHOOL WEEK 3: JOY
ANGELS CELEBRATED JESUS' BIRTH

Items Needed

We're play-acting today. It would be helpful to have the following items available. If that is not possible, just pretend.

- Baby dolls (1 per child)

- Doll blankets or hand towels (1 per child)

- Lambs, sheep, pillows, or stuffed animals (for the shepherd's "flock")

- 1 flashlight (for you to use)

Today's Bible Verses

It may be helpful to look up these verses and bookmark them in advance. Older children and teens can help you.

Don't have a Bible at home? Try http://biblegateway.com. Type the reference below, hit enter, and it will take you right to it.

- Luke 2:7-17a (That means it's just through the first part of verse 17.)

Advent Wreath Candle Guide

Each week, light the previous weeks' candles before moving on to the new one. You may also choose to have the previous weeks' candles already lit and simply light the new one. Once lit, the appropriate candles should burn for the rest of your devotional time. Candles may also be lit at meals or other times.

Today we light the (purple) candle of Hope, the (purple) candle of Peace, and the (PINK) candle of Joy.

Opening Prayer

Dear Lord, thank You for Christmas. Thank You for Jesus. We love you, Lord. Amen.

Think About It

NOTE: I encourage you to start this devotional by sharing your memories of the first day you met the children in your family or group. How did you meet? What else was happening that day? What did they look like? What did you think when you met them? How have they changed since then?

Christmas is an exciting time of year. Whose birthday do we celebrate at Christmas? (Let children answer.)

When Jesus was born, there weren't any Christmas trees. There weren't special lights or Christmas carols. There weren't stockings or presents under the tree. There weren't nativity sets or Christmas programs. There weren't special church services. There wasn't even a birthday party!

Jesus was born in a dirty barn. He didn't even have a bed! He had to sleep in the straw the animals ate. No one knew that a special baby was born.

But God wanted people to know and celebrate that Jesus, God's Son, was born. Who do you think God chose to tell this good news? (Let children answer.)

Let's see if you're right.

Bible Reading

I'm going to need your help as we read the Bible today. We're going to pretend we're part of the story and act it out.

Get your baby doll. Are you ready?

Luke 2:7-17a (NIRV)

"[Mary] gave birth to her first baby. It was a boy." Rock your baby.

"She wrapped him in large strips of cloth." Wrap your baby in a blanket.

"Then she placed him in a manger. That's because there was no guest room where they could stay." Time to put your baby down to sleep.

Ok. Go over to our pretend flock of sheep.

"There were shepherds living out in the fields nearby. It was night, and they were taking care of their sheep." Can you pet a sheep? Aww! They're so cute.

Suddenly, "An angel of the Lord appeared to them. And the glory of the Lord shone around them." Turn on the flashlight and shine it around.

"They were terrified." Show me your scared face.

"But the angel said to them, 'Do not be afraid. I bring you good news.'" Whew! Show me your happy face.

"'It will bring great joy for all the people.'" Can you cheer with me? "Yay!"

"'Today in the town of David a Savior has been born to you. He is the Messiah, the Lord.'" Who is the angel talking about? (Let children answer.)

"'Here is how you will know I am telling you the truth. You will find a baby wrapped in strips of cloth and lying in a manger.'" Show me where your baby is sleeping. (Let children get their babies.) Good. Now put them back down to bed and come back to the sheep.

"Suddenly a large group of angels from heaven also appeared. They were praising God." Everybody say, "Praise God!" ("Praise God!")

The angels "said, 'May glory be given to God in the highest heaven! And may peace be given to those he is pleased with on earth!'"

We're going to sing like the angels. Are you ready? (Sing either "Angels We Have Heard on High," "Praise Him, Praise Him All Ye Little Children," or "Oh How I Love Jesus.")

"The angels left and went into heaven." Wave goodbye.

"Then the shepherds said to one another, 'Let's go to Bethlehem. Let's see this thing that has happened, which the Lord has told us about.'" Go find your baby.

"So they hurried off and found Mary and Joseph and the baby. The baby was lying in the manger." Aww! The baby's so cute. Can you rock your baby?

"After the shepherds had seen him, they told everyone..." Let's practice telling people about Jesus. Say, "Jesus was born at Christmas." (echo)

Now tell your baby. "Jesus was born at Christmas." (echo)

Now tell one of your friends. "Jesus was born at Christmas." (echo)

Now say it really loud so they can hear you outside. "JESUS WAS BORN AT CHRISTMAS!" (echo)

Great job! Now put your baby back to bed. And come sit with me.

Let's see how well you listened.

- Who was the baby boy?

- Who was taking care of the sheep?

- How did the shepherds learn that Jesus was born?

- What did the angels do?

- Did the shepherds do what the angels told them to do?

- After they saw baby Jesus, what did the shepherds do?

Good job!

Suggested Songs

The songs below are considered by some to be standard children's songs. As such, they should be easily available in online videos and audio tracks.

- "Happy Birthday" to Jesus

- "Praise Him, Praise Him All Ye Little Children"

- "I've got the Joy, Joy, Joy Down In My Heart"

- "To God Be the Glory"

Family Fun

Help children practice telling people about Jesus this week. (It's good practice for adults too.) "Jesus was born at Christmas."

Let's practice. First let's say it all together. Ready, "Jesus was born at Christmas." (Repeat as needed.)

Practice saying it one at a time to each other.

Go into each child's room and take turns saying it to that child's toys.

Find pictures or artwork of people in your house and take turns saying it to those "people."

Then talk about who else you can tell.

- Who can you tell at the store?

- Who can you tell on the playground?

- Who can you tell at church?

- Who can you tell in your family?

PRESCHOOL WEEK 4: LOVE
GOD LOVES US

Items Needed

We're playing a game with emotion signs today. It would be helpful to have the following signs ready in advance. You will need 4 pieces of paper and a contrasting colored utensil to draw.

- Sad face

- Mad face

- Glad face

- Scared face

Not feeling very artistic? It doesn't have to be fancy. See the samples below. You could also color code your faces. Sad is blue. Mad is red. Glad is yellow. Scared is white.

Today's Bible Verses

It may be helpful to look up these verses and bookmark them in advance. Older children and teens can help you.

Don't have a Bible at home? Try http://biblegateway.com. Type the reference below, hit enter, and it will take you right to it.

- Romans 8:35, 39

Advent Wreath Candle Guide

Each week, light the previous weeks' candles before moving on to the new one. You may also choose to have the previous weeks' candles already lit and simply light the new one. Once lit, the appropriate candles should burn for the rest of your devotional time. Candles may also be lit at meals or other times.

Today we light the (purple) candle of Hope, the (purple) candle of Peace, the (PINK) candle of Joy, and the (purple) candle of Love.

Opening Prayer

Dear God, thank You for loving us no matter what. We love You too, Jesus. Amen.

Think About It

Sad, mad, glad, and scared are emotions. Sad, mad, glad, and scared are ways we can feel.

I feel sad when I say goodbye to my friends. Show me a sad face. (Do it with the children.) Have you ever felt sad? (Let children share.)

I feel mad when someone takes my things. Show me a mad face. (Do it with the children.) Have you ever felt mad? (Let children share.)

I feel glad when I get my favorite food for supper. Show me a glad face. (Do it with the children.) Have you ever felt glad? (Let children share.)

I feel scared when I go to a new place. (Feel free to supply your own situation.) Show me a scared face. (Do it with the children.) Have you ever felt scared? (Let children share.)

How do you feel when you get ice cream? (Feel free to change "ice cream" to another treat if desired.) Do you feel sad, mad, glad, or scared? (Let children respond.) Show me a ______ (fill in emotion) face. (Do it with the children.)

How do you feel when an adult says it's time to clean up your toys? Do you feel sad, mad, glad, or scared? (Let children respond.) Show me a ______ (fill in emotion) face. (Do it with the children.)

How do you feel when you meet new people? Do you feel sad, mad, glad, or scared? (Let children respond.) Show me a ______ (fill in emotion) face. (Do it with the children.)

How do you feel when your brother or sister (or friend) takes your toy? Do you feel sad, mad, glad, or scared? (Let children respond.) Show me a ______ (fill in emotion) face. (Do it with the children.)

How do you feel when you get in trouble? (Feel free to change "get in trouble" to "go to time out" or another punishment regularly given.) Do you feel sad, mad, glad, or scared? (Let children respond.) Show me a ______ (fill in emotion) face. (Do it with the children.)

How do you feel when you get to play with your friends? (Feel free to name specific friends if desired.) Do you feel sad, mad, glad, or scared? (Let children respond.) Show me a ______ (fill in emotion) face. (Do it with the children.)

Sad, mad, glad, and scared are emotions. Sad, mad, glad, and scared are ways we can feel. God loves us no matter what we feel. God loves us when we're sad. God loves us when we're mad. God loves us when we're glad. God loves us when we're scared. God always loves us, no matter what.

We're going to read the Bible in just a minute. When you hear me say, "God always loves us," I want you to hug yourself and say it back to me: God always loves us. Are you ready to practice? (Hug yourself.) God always loves us. ("God loves us!" Practice this together until the kids are confident.)

Bible Reading
Today we're reading from the New Testament book of Romans, chapter 8, verses 35 and 39 (NIRV).

(hug yourself) God always loves us. ("God always loves us.")

"Who can separate us from Christ's love?" (hug yourself) God always loves us. ("God always loves us.")

(make a mad face) "Can trouble or hard times" (make a sad face) "or harm or hunger?"

(make a scared face) "Can nakedness or danger or war?"

(hug yourself) God always loves us. ("God always loves us.")

(make a glad face) "Not even the highest places or the lowest, or anything else in all creation can separate us.. Nothing at all can ever separate us from God's love. That's because of what Christ Jesus our Lord has done."

(hug yourself) God always loves us. ("God always loves us.")

(make a mad face) Does God love us when we're mad? (Let children answer.)

(hug yourself) God always loves us. ("God always loves us.")

(make a sad face) Does God love us when we're sad? (Let children answer.)

(hug yourself) God always loves us. ("God always loves us.")

(make a scared face) Does God love us when we're scared? (Let children answer.)

(hug yourself) God always loves us. ("God always loves us.")

(make a glad face) Does God love us when we're glad? (Let children answer.)

(hug yourself) God always loves us. ("God always loves us.")

One more time. (hug yourself) God always loves us. ("God always loves us.")

That's right. No matter how we feel, (hug yourself) God always loves us. ("God always loves us.")

Suggested Songs

The songs below are considered by some to be standard children's songs. As such, they should be easily available in online videos and audio tracks.

- "Deep and Wide"

- "Oh How I Love Jesus"

- "Jesus Loves the Little Children"

- "This Is My Commandment"

Family Fun

We're going to play a game. Are you ready? [You will need your emotion signs. See "Items Needed" above.]

Sometimes when I'm glad, I do a happy dance. Can you show me a happy dance? (Don't be shy. Jump in and do it with them.)

Sometimes when I'm mad, I stomp my feet. Can you stomp your feet? (Do it with them.)

Sometimes when I'm sad, I put my hands on my face. Can you put your hands on your face? (Do it with them.)

Sometimes when I'm scared, I jump. Can you jump? (Do it with them.)

(hug yourself) God always loves us. ("God always loves us.")

(Practice this a few times before moving on.)

(Hold up the glad sign.) This is glad face. Can you show me a happy dance? (Do it with them.) Good.

(Hold up the mad sign.) This is a mad face. Can you stomp your feet? (Do it with them.) Good.

(Hold up the sad sign.) This is sad face. Can you cover your face? (Do it with them.) Good.

(Hold up the scared sign.) This is scared face. Can you jump? (Do it with them.) Good.

(hug yourself) God always loves us. ("God always loves us.")

(Practice this a few times before moving on.)

(Hold up the glad sign.) What is this? (Let children answer.) Can you show me a happy dance? (Do it with them.) Good.

(Hold up the mad sign.) What is this? (Let children answer.) Can you stomp your feet? (Do it with them.) Good.

(Hold up the sad sign.) What is this? (Let children answer.) Can you cover your face? (Do it with them.) Good.

(Hold up the scared sign.) What is this? (Let children answer.) Can you jump? (Do it with them.) Good.

(hug yourself) God always loves us. ("God always loves us.")

(Practice this a few times.)

Great job!

PRESCHOOL CHRISTMAS EVE OR CHRISTMAS DAY: CHRIST JESUS IS GOD'S SON

Today's Bible Verses

It may be helpful to look up these verses and bookmark them in advance. Older children and teens can help you.

Don't have a Bible at home? Try http://biblegateway.com. Type the reference below, hit enter, and it will take you right to it.

- Luke 2:1-21. Consider using the New International Readers Version (NIRV).

- Matthew 2:1-12. Consider using the New International Readers Version (NIRV).

Items Needed

We're talking about babies and birthdays today. It would be helpful to have the following available.

- Baby pictures (your children's, yours, or someone else's)

- Baby doll

- Children's nativity set (optional)

Advent Wreath Candle Guide

Each week, light the previous weeks' candles before moving on to the new one. You may also choose to have the previous weeks' candles already lit and simply light the new one. Once lit, the appropriate candles should burn for the rest of your devotional time. Candles may also be lit at meals or other times.

Today we light the four candles from the previous weeks: Hope (purple), Peace (purple), Joy (pink), and Love (purple). Not all advent wreaths have a fifth candle. If you do have a fifth candle, this is the day you light it as well. This is the Christ candle. If your wreath only has four candles, simply light those four.

Opening Prayer

Dear God, thank You for Jesus. Thank You that You love us. Happy birthday, Jesus! We love you. Amen.

Think About It

Christmas is the time we celebrate Jesus' birthday. You were a baby once.

(Get out your baby pictures and tell the stories of the babies in them. Tell about the day you met your children. Tell their birth stories if you know them.)

Some extra special things happened when Jesus was born. Let's read the Bible and see what happened.

Bible Reading

Read Luke 2:1-21 and Matthew 2:1-12. Consider using the New International Readers Version (NIRV). *Be sure to read expressively.*

Family Fun

Ask the kids help you retell the story while you act it out. Use your child-friendly nativity set or follow the instructions below.

For younger preschoolers, everyone should do the same thing at the same time rather than assigning parts. Rather than asking the children to tell you what happened, reread the Bible lesson from Luke 2:1-21 and Matthew 2:1-12.

Characters needed: Angel (one or more), Mary, Joseph, Inn Keeper (optional), a doll for Baby Jesus (or more than one if everyone is going to use it at the same time), Shepherd(s), Sheep (optional), Wise Man (one or more)

Pretend locations needed: Mary's home, Joseph's bed, sheep field, inn (optional), stable, "the East," roads

If you really want to get fancy: You can pull together costumes as well if you like, though they are not necessary.

What to do: Ask the children to tell you what happened, correcting them as needed. Act it out as you go. Have fun!

The songs below are considered by some to be standard children's songs. As such, they should be easily available in online videos and audio tracks.

- "Away in a Manger"

- "Happy Birthday" to Jesus

- "Little Drummer Boy" (This is especially fun if everyone has their own drums to play through the song.)

- Your favorite Christmas carols

Children's Lessons

CHILDREN'S WEEK 1: HOPE

HOPE IN CHRIST IS A KNOW–FOR–SURE KIND OF HOPE

Items Needed

For today's lesson, you will need the following:

- A chair that you trust will hold you when you sit in it

- Either a bottle of bubble solution or cups of water and straws for each person (If you use cups and straws, just blow bubbles in your cup of water.)

- Building blocks

- Three separate places. This could either be three parts of the room or three connected rooms. The goal is to have a place to talk, one to put the bubbles/cups of water that will not be knocked over when using the building blocks area.

Today's Bible Verses

It may be helpful to look up these verses and bookmark them in advance. Older children and teens can help you.

Don't have a Bible at home? Try http://biblegateway.com. Type the reference below, hit enter, and it will take you right to it.

- Hebrews 11:1-2

- Hebrews 11:39-40

- 1 Corinthians 15:3-4

Each week, light the previous weeks' candles before moving on to the new one. You may also choose to have the previous weeks' candles already lit and simply light the new one. Once lit, the appropriate candles should burn for the rest of your devotional time. Candles may also be lit at meals or other times.

Today we start with the candle of Hope (purple if using a multi-colored set).

Opening Prayer
Thank you, Lord, that we can trust in You. Please teach us the difference between wishful hope and trustworthy hope. Thank You that we can always trust You. In Jesus' name we pray, amen.

Think About It
Today we lit a candle that reminds us of hope. What do you think hope mean? (Let children answer, but don't correct them yet.)

Did you know there are two different kinds of hope? One kind of hope is a wish, something we wish would happen. The wish kind of hope might happen or it might not. I could say I hope it rains tomorrow. I can hope all I want, but it might not happen. We see the wish kind of hope a lot at Christmas. For example, what do you hope to get for Christmas? (Let all children answer.)

That is the wish kind of hope.

The other kind of hope is knowing for sure something is going to happen. The know-for-sure kind of hope is when we're looking forward to something we know for sure is going to happen.

What is something you know for sure is going to happen? (Let children answer. It's ok if they can't think of anything.)

Let me show you the know-for-sure kind of hope. (Stand by the chair.) Do you see this chair? If I sit in this chair, do you think it will hold me? Or will it collapse and make me fall on the floor? (Let children answer.) How do you know? (Let children answer.)

I hope it will hold me. I really think it will. I think this is a know-for-sure kind of hope, not a wish kind of hope. Let's see who's right. (Sit in the chair.)

Was I right? Was my hope well founded? (Let children answer.)

Let's play a game to practice the difference between wish hope and know-for-sure hope.

When we say something that is a wish hope, we're going to blow bubbles for five seconds. (Show the area you've chosen for the bubble station.) Are you ready to practice? Ready... Set... Wait for it! Ready... Set... GO! One, two, three, four, STOP! Did we stop on time?

Let's try it one more time. Ready... Set... GO! One, two, three, four, STOP! Did we stop on time? (Practice again if you didn't. Feel free to give another false start if you wish.)

Alright. What kind of hope do we come blow bubbles? (Let kids answer. The correct answer is the wish kind of hope.)

When we say something that is a know-for-sure hope, we're going to build with blocks for five seconds. (Show the area you've chosen for the block station.) You won't have time to build a whole house, so just build as tall of a tower as you can in five seconds. Are you ready to practice? Ready... Set... Wait for it! Ready... Set... GO! One, two, three, four, STOP! Did we stop on time?

Let's try it one more time. Ready... Set... GO! One, two, three, four, STOP! Did we stop on time? (Practice again if you didn't. Feel free to give another false start if you wish.)

Alright. What kind of hope do we come build a tower? (Let kids answer. The correct answer is the know-for-sure kind of hope.)

Are you ready to play?

Here's the first one: What kind of hope is this? I hope I get a pony for Christmas. (Name the kind of hope, then run to the correct station.) Ready... Set... GO! One, two, three, four, STOP!

Next one: What kind of hope is this? I hope the stars shine at night. (Name the kind of hope, then run to the correct station.) Ready... Set... GO! One, two, three, four, STOP!

Next question: What kind of hope is this? I hope we have a white Christmas. (Name the kind of hope, then run to the correct station.) Ready... Set... GO! One, two, three, four, STOP!

Next: What kind of hope is this? I hope God loves me. (Name the kind of hope, then run to the correct station.) Ready... Set... GO! One, two, three, four, STOP!

Next: What kind of hope is this? I hope I get an A on my test. (Name the kind of hope, then run to the correct station.) Ready... Set... GO! One, two, three, four, STOP!

Next: What kind of hope is this? I hope my jacket and scarf keep me warm. (Name the kind of hope, then run to the correct station.) Ready... Set... GO! One, two, three, four, STOP!

Next: What kind of hope is this? I hope New Year's comes after Christmas. (Name the kind of hope, then run to the correct station.) Ready... Set... GO! One, two, three, four, STOP!

Just three more: What kind of hope is this? I hope when I flip the light switch that the light turns on. (Name the kind of hope, then run to the correct station.) Ready... Set... GO! One, two, three, four, STOP!

Two more: What kind of hope is this? I hope they sing my favorite song in church this Sunday. (Name the kind of hope, then run to the correct station.) Ready... Set... GO! One, two, three, four, STOP!

Last one: Are you ready? What kind of hope is this? I hope what the Bible says is true. (Name the kind of hope, then run to the correct station.) Ready... Set... GO! One, two, three, four, STOP!

Alright. Let's go finish our Bible study.

Bible Reading
Read Hebrews 11:1-2.

What is faith? (Let children answer. Reread Hebrews 11:1 if needed.)

What kind of hope is this verse talking about, the wish hope or the know-for-sure hope? (Let children answer.)

The rest of this chapter lists a whole bunch of people from the Old Testament who trusted God and lived for Him. People like Noah, Abraham, Joseph, Moses, Samuel, and David.

Then the Bible says something interesting. Read Hebrews 11:39-40.

God promised these people that one day Jesus would come. They had faith that God would keep His promise. None of them were alive long enough to meet Jesus face to face, but they had faith and hope that God would keep His promise. What kind of hope is that? (Let children answer.)

When Jesus came, He showed that God always keeps His promises. There are at least 353 prophecies about Jesus. These are all promises God made about Jesus before He was born. Jesus fulfilled every single one.

Read 1 Corinthians 15:3-4.

We can have the know-for-sure hope that God will always keep His promises because God already proved that He always keeps His promises.

Closing Prayer
Thank you, Lord, that we can trust in You. Thank You for always keeping Your promises. Teach us to have faith and hope in You. In Jesus' name we pray, amen.

The songs below are considered by some to be standard children's songs. As such, they should be easily available in online videos and audio tracks.

- "I Want a Hippopotamus for Christmas" (wish kind of hope)

- "O Come, O Come Emmanuel" (know-for-sure kind of hope)

CHILDREN'S WEEK 2: PEACE
WHAT DOES PEACE MEAN?

Items Needed

For today's lesson, you will need the following:

- Paper

- Art supplies (crayons, markers, paint and brushes, or other creative supplies)

Today's Bible Verses

It may be helpful to look up these verses and bookmark them in advance. Older children and teens can help you.

Don't have a Bible at home? Try http://biblegateway.com. Type the reference below, hit enter, and it will take you right to it.

- Luke 2:14 (quoted below)

- John 16:33

- Philippians 4:4-8

- Psalm 139:3-4, 11-12 (optional)

- Isaiah 59:2

- 1 John 1:9

- Romans 10:9-10

- Philippians 1:6 (optional)

- Romans 12 (optional)

- James 5:16

- Philippians 4:4-9

Advent Wreath Candle Guide

Each week, light the previous weeks' candles before moving on to the new one. You may also choose to have the previous weeks' candles already lit and simply light the new one. Once lit, the appropriate candles should burn for the rest of your devotional time. Candles may also be lit at meals or other times.

Today we light two candles: last week's candle of Hope and this week's candle of Peace (both are purple if using a multi-colored set).

Opening Prayer

Thank You that You are in charge of everything. Thank You, God, for giving us peace. We give you glory today. We love You, Lord. In Jesus' name we pray, amen.

Think About It

Peace is the calm feeling you have inside when you know things are going to be ok.

We hear that word "peace" a lot a Christmas. "Peace on earth and good will to men." That comes from the Bible. When Jesus was born, angels told the shepherds and praised God. They said, "May glory[4] be given to God in the highest heaven! And may peace be given to those he is pleased with on earth!"[5] (Luke 2:14 NIRV).

Where else have you heard the word "peace"? (Let children answer if they can.) Sometimes I hear the phrase "peace and quiet."

Peace is the calm feeling you have inside when you know things are going to be ok. The opposite of peace is worry, fear, anger, war, or chaos.

Tell me about a time you were worried, afraid, or angry. (Let children answer.)

Tell me about a time you felt at peace. (Let children answer.)

Family Fun

Give each person one piece of paper and put out the art supplies.

Show children how to fold the paper in half. It doesn't matter if the paper is folded "hotdog" (long and skinny) or "hamburger" (short and fat) style.

---

[4] Wonder what glory is too? The *Baker Encyclopedia of the Bible* defines "the Glory of God" like this: "The glory of God can be described in two senses: (1) as a general category or attribute, and (2) as a specific category referring to particular historical manifestations of his presence." Dillard, R. B. 1988. "Glory." In *Baker Encyclopedia of the Bible*. Vol. 1. Grand Rapids, MI: Baker Book House, p. 870.

[5] The difference in wording has to do with the translation's goal to convey the original meaning of the Greek text. Even so, different English translations have slightly different meanings. The traditional KJV "and on earth peace, good will toward men" reflects an outdated understanding of how the Greek words in this verse fit together. A better understanding of what the original Greek text says would be, "and on earth there is peace among the people whom God has favored." Nolland, J. 2002. *Word Biblical Commentary*. Vol. 35A. *Luke 1:1–9:20*. Dallas: Word, Incorporated, p. 97, 102.

Open the paper.

Peace is the calm feeling you have inside when you know things are going to be ok. On one half, make a picture of what it feels like to have peace.

On the other half, make a picture of what it feels like to have the opposite of peace (anger, fear, or war).

(You may need to continue with the Bible Reading while children finish, especially if you have one child that finishes quickly and one child that must finish every detail.)

Bible Reading

If we sin, peace is impossible. Sin, disobedience, and not doing what God asks of us blocks our prayers. It also blocks the work of the Holy Spirit in our lives.

Read Isaiah 59:2.

The first step to peace is to follow the Holy Spirit's leading by believing in Jesus and asking God to forgive us.

Read 1 John 1:9 and Romans 10:9-10.

When we follow the Holy Spirit's leading and ask Jesus to be our Lord and Savior, He wipes away all our sin like it never happened. We may still have to face consequences in our relationships with other people, but God sees us like we never sinned in the first place. I wish I could tell you that from that point on we never sin. That is not the case. God continues to work in our lives, making us more like Jesus as we follow Him, but we will not be perfect until we get to heaven (Philippians 1:6; Romans 12).

We all still mess up and sin. That sin blocks our prayers and stops the work of the Holy Spirit in our lives. The solution is to confess our sin to God and to those we sinned against. Confession is simply telling on yourself, saying you are sorry, and meaning it. In our lying example, you would need to confess to the adult who asked if your homework was finished.

Read James 5:16.

Confession is the first step to peace, but God tells us even more about how to live in His peace. As we read this next set of verses, listen for things we can do to get peace.

Read Philippians 4:4-9.

- What are things we can do to get peace? (Reread the passage as necessary.)

- That stuff isn't always easy. What can you do to remind yourself to do these things?

Take some time to develop a plan of action, asking yourself the following questions:

- When is it hard to remember to do these things?

- What can I do in those moments to remind myself what God says?

- What other things can I change about the way I do certain things that would help me avoid tough situations? (For example, could you pack your backpack after supper so you know you have everything ready for the next day?)

Closing Prayer

Lord, You are so amazing! Please continue to teach us more about You. When we are worried, scared, upset, or angry, teach us to pray and ask You for peace. Help us to remember that we can have peace, feeling calm inside, knowing that everything is going to be ok because You are in charge. Thank You, God, that You are always with us. In Jesus' name we pray, amen.

Suggested Songs
- "Silent Night"

- "It Came Upon the Midnight Clear"

CHILDREN'S WEEK 3: JOY
GOOD NEWS OF GREAT JOY!

Items Needed

For today's activity, we are making a Christmas wreath with a cross on it. You may choose to make a larger one for your family or smaller ones for each person. You will need the following:

- One cross per wreath per wreath (various sizes can be found at craft stores or you can cut them out of yellow construction paper or foam sheet)

- Either (1) an evergreen wreath, (2) cutouts of a wreath on green construction paper, or (3) cutouts of a wreath on green foam sheets [Not feeling artistic? For a simple wreath, cut circles about the size of a bowl. Then cut out a second circle from the middle about the size of a cup. You should be left with a donut shape.)

- Ribbons, stars, and other decorations (stickers work great for cutout wreaths)

- Evergreen sprigs (if using construction paper or foam sheets)

- Glue (Hot glue or crafting wire works best on evergreen wreaths. Glue dots or school glue works best on cutout wreaths.)

- OPTIONAL: the letters J, O, Y

Today's Bible Verses

It may be helpful to look up these verses and bookmark them in advance. Older children and teens can help you.

Don't have a Bible at home? Try http://biblegateway.com. Type the reference below, hit enter, and it will take you right to it.

- Luke 2:1-20

This is a longer lesson, so I recommend looking up the following verses in advance or another time. They are referred to in parentheses below.

- Matthew 11:4-5

- Hebrews 4:15

- Romans 6:23
- John 3:14-18
- Acts 13:27-33
- 1 Peter 1:3-5

- Romans 10:9-10
- Romans 3:22-24
- Mark 1:15

Advent Wreath Candle Guide

Each week, light the previous weeks' candles before moving on to the new one. You may also choose to have the previous weeks' candles already lit and simply light the new one. Once lit, the appropriate candles should burn for the rest of your devotional time. Candles may also be lit at meals or other times.

Today we light the (purple) candle of Hope, the (purple) candle of Peace, and the (PINK) candle of Joy.

Opening Prayer

Dear Lord, please teach us to seek joy in every situation. Fix our eyes on Jesus so we focus on You and not what is happening around us. Give us endurance and grow our faith. In Jesus' name we pray, amen.

Think About It

What are some things that make you happy? (Let children answer.)

People often mix up "happy" and "joy" thinking they are the same things. Take a guess. What do you think is the difference between "happy" and "joyful"? (Let children take a guess.)

Happy is an emotion. We feel happy when good things happen. A happy feeling does not last. We are happy for a little while, but then it goes away.

Joy is an attitude. It is a choice. No matter what emotion we are feeling, we can choose to be joyful. We do that by turning our focus to things that never change. We focus on Jesus and God's promises. We will talk more about that later, but for now, let's think again about the difference between joy and happy.

Joy is like evergreen leaves. We see a lot of evergreen around Christmas time. Christmas trees are evergreen trees. They are called evergreen because the leaves stay green. Well, unless the tree dies. Then they turn yellow. But a live evergreen tree always has green leaves that look like needles. Sometimes evergreen trees are hard to find. Sometimes snow or fog may cover up the leaves so we can't see them. But even then, the evergreen needles are still there and still green. We just may have to look harder to find them. Like the green on evergreen leaves, we can always find joy because it depends on God's promises.

Happy, on the other hand, is sometimes there and sometimes it goes away. Happy is like leaves on deciduous trees (like aspen, oak, or maple). Their green leaves show up in the spring and are there for the summer, but in the fall they change colors and fall off the tree. The tree is then bare. The tree is still alive, but the leaves are all gone. It stays that way all winter. Like deciduous leaves, happy is sometimes there and sometimes it is gone because happy is an emotion.

Let's review. Like the green on evergreen leaves, we can always find joy because it depends on God's promises. Like deciduous leaves, happy is sometimes there and sometimes it is gone because happy is an emotion.

- Which one is sometimes there and sometimes not? (Happy.)
- Which one is always there? (Joy.)
- Why is happy sometimes there and sometimes not? (Because emotions change.)
- Why is joy always there? (Because it depends on God's promises.)

Family Fun
Gather your Christmas wreath supplies and get creative. Make a Christmas wreath you like. Be sure to include a cross. Remember, like the green on evergreen leaves, we can always find joy because it depends on God's promises.

Bible Reading
Open your Bible to Luke 2:1-20. As we read today, only the person reading aloud will have their eyes open. Everyone else, close your eyes. Pretend you are experiencing these thing as they happened for the first time. Think about what you see, what you hear, what you smell, and what you feel. Put yourself in the story. Are you ready?

Read Luke 2:1-20.

Tell me what happened. (Allow children to share and ask questions. Know that if a question stumps you, it's ok to say "I don't know.")

The angels brought "good news of great joy" to the shepherds. Do you remember what it was? (Review Luke 2:10-12 as needed.)

A Savior. This new baby was supposed to be a Savior who is Christ the Lord. A savior is someone who saves someone else. Let's look at how Jesus is our Savior.

If you already know how, this is a good chance for you to remember the amazing things Jesus did for you. Listen and thank God for Jesus. Think about who you could tell about Jesus this Christmas.

We celebrate Jesus' birth at Christmas, but Jesus didn't stay a baby. He grew to be a child like you and then an adult. When He was all grown up, Jesus healed the blind, the sick, and people who couldn't walk (Matthew 11:4-5).

Jesus also taught people about sin and God's love. Sin is the wrong choices we make. Sin is anything we think, say, do, or don't do that breaks God's perfect standard. We know that no one is perfect. Romans 3:23 says that everyone has sinned at least once--everyone except Jesus (Hebrews 4:15). Romans 6:23 says that the punishment for sin is death. This is a problem because the death in the Bible can also mean being separated from God and all the good things He is and gives. This is a problem, but God in His love provided the answer (John 3:14-18).

Even though Jesus healed people and did all kinds of good things, not everyone liked Him. Jesus' enemies finally had Him arrested and killed. Jesus died on a cross like the one on our wreaths. That is sad, but here's the "good news of great joy" the angels sang about. When Jesus died, He took the punishment for our sins. And Jesus didn't stay dead! Jesus' friends buried Him in a cave and rolled a big stone over the entrance to seal it. Three days later, Jesus came back to life again! This was proof that God accepted Jesus' payment for our sins (Acts 13:27-33).

Now God offers us a gift better than anything under the tree. If we agree with God that we've messed up and sinned and we believe that Jesus is who He said He was and did what the Bible says He did, then we will be saved. God forgives all of the things we've done wrong and comes to live with us every day of our life. When we die, we'll get to go to heaven to live with God (1 Peter 1:3-5).

Here's the catch. God offers this gift of salvation through Jesus to everybody. But, we have to follow the Holy Spirit's leading and accept that gift before it is ours (Romans 10:9-10). Think of it like a Christmas gift. Let's pretend I made this wreath to give to you. (Hold a wreath in your hand.) Is it yours while I still have it? (Let family members answer. The answer's no.) When is it really yours? (Let family members answer. The answer is when that person takes it.)

God offers us salvation through Jesus Christ. The Holy Spirit works in our hearts, leading us to accept Jesus as our Lord and Savior. We accept that gift by telling God we agree that we've done bad things and are truly sorry for them. We must then believe that Jesus is who the Bible says He is and that He died and came back to life again. Then God forgives us and comes to live with us. Out of our love for God and joy, we then try to live in a way that honors God (Romans 3:22-24; Mark 1:15).

Have you ever done that? (Let children answer. Help those who desire it to pray, confessing sin and asking Jesus to save them. Don't worry or push if kids aren't ready yet. Just give the Holy Spirit more time to work in their hearts as they ask questions and keep learning.)

Closing Prayer
Thank You God for Jesus. Thank You for the "good news of great joy" that the angels brought to the shepherds. Help us keep looking for You. Give us joy as we remember what Jesus did for us. In Christ's name we pray, amen.

Suggested Songs

- "Joy to the World"

- "Go Tell It On the Mountain"

- "Angels We Have Heard on High"

CHILDREN'S WEEK 4: LOVE
GOD'S LOVE IS UNCONDITIONAL

Items Needed

You will need the following:

- A whiteboard or scrap paper (A whiteboard is preferred, but either is fine.)

- Appropriate pens (Please make sure they work.)

- Whiteboard eraser (optional)

Today's Bible Verses

It may be helpful to look up these verses and bookmark them in advance. Older children and teens can help you.

Don't have a Bible at home? Try http://biblegateway.com. Type the reference below, hit enter, and it will take you right to it.

- 1 John 4:9-10

- Romans 5:8 (quoted below)

- 1 John 4:11-12 (optional)

This is a longer lesson, so I recommend looking up the following verses in advance or another time. They are referred to in parentheses below.

- Genesis 1-3

- 1 Samuel 2:2

- Luke 2

- John 1

- Hebrews 4:15

- Matthew 26:36-28:20

- John 1:12; 3:16

- Romans 6:23; 10:9-10

- Ephesians 2:1-10

Advent Wreath Candle Guide

Each week, light the previous weeks' candles before moving on to the new one. You may also choose to have the previous weeks' candles already lit and simply light the new one. Once lit, the appropriate candles should burn for the rest of your devotional time. Candles may also be lit at meals or other times.

Today we light the (purple) candle of Hope, the (purple) candle of Peace, the (PINK) candle of Joy, and the (purple) candle of Love.

Opening Prayer

God, You are amazing! The Bible says that You are love. Thank You for Your great love. Please teach us how to love You more. Teach us how to love other people the way You love us. In Jesus' name we pray, amen.

Think About It

What are some things that you love? (Encourage each family member to share one to three things.)

Did you know that there are different kinds of love?

One kind of love is the mushy "Mommy and Daddy" kind of love. In Greek it's called *eros* (AIR-oh-s) love. Let's call it "Mom and Dad" love. Say that with me: "Mom and Dad love." (Repeat as necessary.)

A second kind of love is the "you're my good friend" kind of love. In Greek it's called *philos* (fih-lay-oh) love. The city of Philadelphia, PA, is called the City of Brotherly Love because the name Philadelphia has the word *philos*[6] in it. "Brotherly love" is another way to say it's a "good friend" love. Say that with me: "good friend love." (Repeat as necessary.)

- Who would you say you "good friend" love? (Let family members answer.)

A third kind of love is the "favorite food" kind of love. I don't know a Greek word for that, so let's call it "favorite" love. Say that with me: "favorite love." (Repeat as necessary.)

- What is one thing that you would say you "favorite" love? (Let family members answer.)

---

[6] Are you trying to find all of the letters of *phileo* in the name Philadelphia? It doesn't work that way. Philadelphia is a compound word. In Greek that means some letters drop out. "Phil" is all that is left from *philos*. *Adelphos* means "brother," but that ending is also changed slightly in this compound word. Isn't it funny that the name says the same thing twice? It's like the name of the city is actually "brotherly love for my brother" or "good friend love for my brothers and sisters" (the sisters are implied). Pretty cool!

A fourth kind of love is the "love you no matter what" kind of love. It's also called unconditional love. In Greek it's called *agape* (uh-gah-pay) love. This is the kind of love God has for us. God is our perfect Father. He shows us how to love other people, especially our families, no matter what.

(If your children have experienced a less than perfect home life, be sure to emphasize that God is our *perfect* Father. Earthly fathers and mothers are supposed to follow God's example and love their kids no matter what. Unfortunately, our earthly fathers and mothers aren't perfect and make mistakes. Even so, God shows us what real love looks like as our perfect Father. We can follow His example and love other people the way God loves us.)

God's love is unconditional. It is "no matter what" love. Say that with me: "God's love is unconditional. It is 'no matter what' love." (Repeat as necessary.)

What if I mess up? Would God still love me then? (Let family members answer.)

What if I fall down and get really hurt? Would God still love me then? (Let family members answer.)

What if I hurt somebody? Would God still love me then? (Let family members answer.)

What if I get caught telling a really big lie? Would God still love me then? (Let family members answer.)

God's love is unconditional. It is "no matter what" love. Say that with me: "God's love is unconditional. It is 'no matter what' love." (Repeat as necessary.)

Family Fun

Today we're going to play a game where we're going to try to guess some of the things you love.

Take turns drawing pictures on the whiteboard or paper. The person drawing may not speak or use sound effects. Everyone else tries to guess what they are drawing. When the correct answer is given, decide together what kind of love it is: "Mom and Dad" love, "good friend" love, "favorite" love, or unconditional ("no matter what") love. Then it's the next person's turn.

Bible Reading

Let's see how God shows His love for us. Read 1 John 4:9-10.

There are some big words in verse 10. Some translations say Jesus was the "atoning sacrifice" while others say He was the "propitiation for our sins." Do you want to guess what that means? (Let children guess.) To understand what this means, we have to rewind and get some background information.

God made the world and everything in it (Genesis 1-2). God made everything good and perfect like He is perfect (Genesis 1:31; 1 Samuel 2:2).

Since God made everything, He makes the rules. He gave Adam and Eve, the first man and woman, one rule: don't eat from the tree in the middle of the garden where they lived (Genesis 2:16-17). God didn't make people to be robots who had no choice. The love of a robot doesn't mean anything, because they have no choice but to do what they are programed to do. Let's pretend to be robots and say together, "No robot love." Ready? "No robot love." (Repeat if you like.)

God didn't want people's robot love. God wanted people to *choose* to love and obey Him. Unfortunately, Adam and Eve chose to disobey God, break His rule, and sin (Genesis 3:1-6). This broke God's perfect creation. Sin also has consequences. When Adam and Eve chose to sin, death entered the world for the first time (Genesis 3:21, see also verses 19, 22-24; Romans 6:23). They had to leave the beautiful, perfect garden to work hard for their food (Genesis 3:19, 22-24). There were now things that caused humans pain and suffering (Genesis 3:16-19). God's relationship with humans was broken as well as the relationships between people (Genesis 3:16, 22-24).

The world is still broken today. What are some ways you see that the world is broken and no longer perfect? (Let family members answer.)

Sin is anything we think, say, do, or don't do that goes against what God told us to do. Can you name some sins? (Examples may include hitting a sibling or friend, taking a toy that does not belong to you, or lying.)

People try lots of this to try to fix this brokenness. What are some people try to make things better? (Let family members answer. Possible responses include: punishing themselves, trying to be a good person, going to church a lot, following a list of rules, giving money to good causes, doing things for other people, etc.)

The bad news is that the stuff people try to do can't fix our sin problem. Only God can fix it. The good news is that God loves us unconditionally, no matter what. Romans 5:8 says, "But God demonstrates his own love for us in this: While we were still sinners, Christ died for us" (NIV).

That brings us back to "propitiation" or Jesus' "atoning sacrifice for sin." We couldn't fix our sin problem on our own. Only God could do that. So, God sent His Son Jesus to be born as a human baby (John 1; Luke 2). He grew up to be a man and never sinned, not even once! He never sinned in what He thought, what He said, or what He did, and He never didn't do what He was supposed to do (Hebrews 4:15). Jesus lived a perfect life, but some people hated Him. They killed Him by nailing Him to a cross (Matthew 26:36-27:56). When Jesus died, He didn't have to pay for His sins because He didn't have any. Jesus' death payed the penalty for our sins (Romans 5:17).

Are you ready for the best part? Jesus didn't stay dead! His friends buried Him in a cave and sealed Him in. Then, on the third day, Jesus came back to life again (Matthew 27:57-28:20)! Now we have another choice:

1. We can believe that Jesus is who He said He is and did what the Bible says He did.

2. We can keep asking questions to see if it is true.

3. We can say it's not true and we don't believe.

If we *do* believe, we can tell God we're sorry for our sins (and mean it!) and that we believe in Jesus. Then we will be saved and God will forgive all the things we've done wrong (John 1:12; 3:16; Romans 10:9-10).

When we say that Jesus took our punishment for sin so that God can forgive our sins like they never happened, that is "propitiation" or Jesus' "atoning sacrifice for sin." Atoning sacrifice means making the payment so our sins are wiped away like writing erased from a whiteboard. Propitiation means the same thing. Jesus took our punishment so that if we believe in Him and tell God we're truly sorry for our sins, we will be forgiven.

Have you done that? If not, is the Holy Spirit leading you to do that today? What is stopping you from believing in Jesus and repenting of sin? (NOTE: If one of your family members cannot name some sins and/or does not think he or she has ever sinned, do not push them to say the right answers like a robot. They just aren't ready yet to ask Jesus to be their Lord and Savior. Give the Holy Spirit more time to work on their hearts while they keep asking questions.)

God loves us unconditionally, no matter what. That is why He sent Jesus to take our punishment for sin. We love other people and do nice things for them because God loved us first (Ephesians 2:1-10). (If your children aren't at the end of their attention span, read 1 John 4:11-12.)

Closing Prayer
Thank You, Lord, for Your great love. Thank You for giving up Your life for me. Please teach me to love like You love. Teach me to better show others Your love. In Jesus' name we pray, amen.

Suggested Songs
- "O Come All Ye Faithful"

- "Away in a Manger"

- "Deck the Halls" (Christmas celebrates God's gift of Jesus. Let's celebrate together.)

CHILDREN'S CHRISTMAS EVE OR CHRISTMAS DAY: CHRIST

WHO IS JESUS?

Christmas Alternative

Today's lesson focuses on who Jesus is. If you would rather do this lesson another day and focus on Jesus' birth today, please simply read the following verses together.

Don't have a Bible at home? Try http://biblegateway.com. Type the reference below, hit enter, and it will take you right to it.

- Luke 2:1-21.

- Matthew 2:1-12.

Items Needed

For today's lesson, you will need the following:

- Write the following categories on index cards, scrap paper, or a white board.

    o   Good Man

    o   Wise Teacher

    o   Prophet

    o   Lord

- OPTIONAL: Provide additional writing utensils and index cards/scrap paper/white board space to add the appropriate Scripture references later.

Today's Bible Verses

Here are the verses for today's lesson. It may be helpful to look up these verses and bookmark them in advance. Older children and teens can help you.

Don't have a Bible at home? Try http://biblegateway.com. Type the reference below, hit enter, and it will take you right to it.

- Mark 8:27-28
- Matthew 4:17
- Luke 23:13-15
- Matthew 7:28-29

- John 10:27-30
- John 14:6
- Hebrews 9:14 (optional)
- Luke 18:18-19 (optional)

This is a longer lesson, so I recommend looking up the following verses in advance or another time. They are referred to in parentheses below.

- Acts 1:1-11 (referred to below)
- 2 Peter 1:16 (referred to below)
- 1 Corinthians 15:3-8 (referred to below)
- Mark 8:29 (quoted below)

- Romans 10:9-10 (referred to below)
- James 1:8 (referred to below)
- John 14:25-26 (referred to below)

Advent Wreath Candle Guide

Each week, light the previous weeks' candles before moving on to the new one. You may also choose to have the previous weeks' candles already lit and simply light the new one. Once lit, the appropriate candles should burn for the rest of your devotional time. Candles may also be lit at meals or other times.

Today we light the four candles from the previous weeks: Hope (purple), Peace (purple), Joy (pink), and Love (purple). Not all advent wreaths have a fifth candle. If you do have a fifth candle, this is the day you light it as well. This is the Christ candle. If your wreath only has four candles, simply light those four.

Opening Prayer

Merry Christmas, Lord! Thank You for Jesus. Thank You for a day to celebrate Christ's birth with You and the angels. This Christmas, please show us more clearly who Jesus really is. In Christ's name we pray, amen.

Think About It

If you went out to Walmart and took a survey asking a bunch of different people who Jesus was, you'd get a bunch of different answers. Some people think Jesus was a just a good man or a wise teacher or even a prophet. Some say Jesus is God and should be followed and obeyed as Lord.

This confusion about Jesus is not new. Even when Jesus lived here on earth people had lots of opinions about who He was.

One of the best ways to figure this out is to look at what Jesus said about Himself.

When Jesus lived on this earth, He asked twelve men to hang out with Him all the time. These men were called the disciples. The disciples followed Jesus around, lived in the same places He did, ate meals with Him, watched what He did, and listened to what He said. During the three years they did this, Jesus taught them many things. Jesus also taught other people who followed Him as much as they could. After Jesus died, came back to life, and ascended into heaven (Acts 1:1-11), Jesus' disciples taught other people about Jesus what Jesus said and did.

God also gave them the words to say to write down what they knew about Jesus (2 Timothy 3:16-17;). The Gospels (Matthew, Mark, Luke, and John) are the first four books of the New Testament. They tell us about Jesus' life here on earth. The rest of the New Testament includes references and explanations of what Jesus said and did, but the Gospels simply tell us what happened during Jesus life on earth.

The Gospels were written while people who still knew Jesus were still alive (2 Peter 1:16; 1 Corinthians 15:5-8). That means that if the writer got something wrong, these people would have said something and corrected them. That also means that the writings about Jesus which included made up stuff would not have been included in the Bible. Those who knew better would have made sure the early churches knew they were wrong so that people wouldn't believe a lie. At the end of their lives, the disciples were told they had to either change their stories about Jesus or die. They wouldn't agree, so they died. The disciples died because they knew what they taught about Jesus was true. No one would die trying to protect a lie.

Peter was one of those disciples. He said, "For we did not follow cleverly devised myths when we made known to you the power and coming of our Lord Jesus Christ, but we were eyewitnesses of his majesty" (2 Peter 1:16 ESV).

(To study this topic further, I recommend Lee Strobel's *Case for Christ*. It comes in a technical, adult version, a student version, and a children's version.)

Today we're going to look and see what these eyewitnesses said about Jesus.

Family Fun

Today we're going to play "Who Am I?" Here's how it works. We'll take turns acting out a certain person. You can say things that person would say and act the way that person would act, but you cannot say the person's name. That is what everyone else is going to try to guess.

(HINT: It may be helpful to narrow down the possibilities by choosing a category like the following: sports figures, movie characters, actors, book characters, Bible people, church leaders.)

When finished playing (or during a break), ask: How do you know who the person is? (Let children answer.) We know Jesus is the Christ, the promised Messiah, because His words and actions have been recorded by people who knew Him during His time here on earth.

Bible Reading

Today's Bible reading is going to be a little different. We're going to match up the Bible verses we read with descriptions of Jesus to see who He really was. (Point out your four categories.)

Lord means that Jesus is the boss. Lord means we should listen to what Jesus says and obey Him.

As we read each verse, tell me where you think it best fits. (Read the following verses one at a time. Some may fit in more than one category.)

- Mark 8:27-28
- Matthew 4:17
- Luke 23:13-15
- Matthew 7:28-29

- John 10:27-30
- John 14:6
- Hebrews 9:14 (optional challenge verse)
- Luke 18:18-19 (optional challenge verse)

These are just a few of the things the Bible says about Jesus. Based on these things, was Jesus a good man? (Let children answer.) Was He only a good man and nothing else? (Let children answer)

Was Jesus a wise teacher? (Let children answer.) Was He only a good teacher and nothing else? (Let children answer.)

Was Jesus a prophet? (Let children answer.) Was He only a prophet and nothing else? (Let children answer.)

What does Lord mean again? (Let children answer. Review as needed.) Is Jesus Lord? (Let children answer.) Is He only Lord and nothing else? (Let children answer.)

What else do we know about Jesus? (Let children answer.)

Jesus once asked His disciples an important question. Mark 8:29 says, "And He continued by questioning them, 'But who do you say that I am?' Peter answered and said to Him, 'You are the Christ'" (NASB). The same question applies to us. Who do you say Jesus is? Don't answer out loud, just think about it.

Who Jesus is doesn't change just because we want it to be different. Still, what we believe about Jesus is very important. Only by believing that Jesus is Lord will we be saved (Romans 10:9-10). It's also ok if you're not sure yet what you think about Jesus. God tells us to keep asking questions and He will continue to show us the answers (James 1:5; John 14:25-26). Let's pray and ask God to do that right now.

Closing Prayer

Thank You, God, for Jesus. Thank You that He did so much for us. Teach us to better understand Jesus as Lord. Continue to teach us more about You and answer our questions. In Jesus' name we pray, amen.

Suggested Songs

- "You Shall Call His Name Jesus"

- "The First Noel"

- "We Wish You A Merry Christmas"

- "Happy Birthday" to Jesus

Preteen Lessons

PRETEEN WEEK 1: HOPE

WE CAN HOPE AND TRUST IN CHRIST

Items Needed

For today's lesson, you will need the following:

- A chair that you trust will hold you when you sit in it

- A camera (If none is available, take pretend pictures.)

Today's Bible Verses

It may be helpful to look up these verses and bookmark them in advance. Older children and teens can help you.

Don't have a Bible at home? Try http://biblegateway.com. Type the reference below, hit enter, and it will take you right to it.

- 1 Corinthians 15:1-8

- John 1:12 (optional hint)

- 2 Peter 1:16-21 (optional hint)

- Acts 3:18-26

Why are we doing this?

You are growing physically, mentally, and emotionally. That means you are old enough to ask God tough questions. You are also starting to learn that not everyone thinks the way you do or believes the same things.

You will soon learn, if you haven't already, that there are many people who say there is no reason to believe that Jesus is who He said He is. They say there is no reason to hope and trust in Christ because it is all made up.

It is a good idea to take a closer look at what you believe and why. God said, "Call to Me and I will answer you, and I will tell you great and mighty things, which you do not know" (Jeremiah 33:3 NASB). Again in James 1:5 it says, "But if any of you lacks wisdom, let him ask of God, who gives to all generously and without reproach, and it will be given to him" (NASB).

Let's do that today.

Advent Wreath
(Each week, light the previous weeks' candles before moving on to the new one. You may also choose to have the previous weeks' candles already lit and simply light the new one. Once lit, the appropriate candles should burn for the rest of your devotional time. Candles may also be lit at meals or other times.)

Today we start with the candle of Hope (purple if using a multi-colored set).

Opening Prayer
Dear Lord, thank You for hope. Please show us where our hopes are wishes that may or may not come true. Show us what is true and what is not so we can have the know-for-sure kind of hope. Give us wisdom and clear direction. In Jesus' name we pray, amen.

Different Kinds of Hope
There are two kinds of hope. One is a wish kind of hope. We see this a lot at Christmas. For example, what do you hope to get for Christmas? (Let everyone answer.)

That is the wish kind of hope. It is a wish that may or may not happen.

Today we're talking about the know-for-sure kind of hope. This is a solid hope that something you know for sure is going to happen will happen in the future. Let me show you.

(Stand by the chair.) Do you see this chair? If I sit in this chair, do you think it will hold me? Or will it collapse and make me fall on the floor? (Let everyone answer.) How do you know? (Let everyone answer.)

I hope it will hold me. I think it will. I think this is a know-for-sure kind of hope, not a wish kind of hope. Let's see if my hope was grounded in the truth. (Sit in the chair.)

Today we're going to see if hope and trust in Christ is a wish kind of hope or a know-for-sure kind of hope.

- "O Come, O Come Emmanuel"

- "It's Beginning to Look a Lot Like Christmas"

Bible Reading

Read 1 Corinthians 15:1-8.

- What is the Gospel? (Hint: Read v. 3-4 and John 1:12.)

- How can we be saved? (Hint: Read v. 1-2 and John 1:12.)

- What phrase is repeated in verses 3-4?

- What other witnesses are there that what is written about Jesus is true? (Hint: Read v. 5-8 and 2 Peter 1:16-21.)

Jesus lived, died, and rose again "according to the Scriptures." Today we're going to look at some of those prophecies about Jesus.

Not long after Jesus died and rose again, Peter gave a sermon where he explained the way Jesus fulfilled two prophecies given to Abraham and Moses. Read Acts 3:18-26.

- What did Moses say about Jesus?

- What did God say to Abraham about Jesus?

Think About It

Let's look at how long God's people had to wait, trusting and hoping in the promises of the Messiah to come.

Abraham lived about 2,000 B.C.[7] God promised the Messiah would be a descendant of Abraham through whom all nations would be blessed (Genesis 12:3).

Moses led the children of Israel out of Egypt in either 1440 or 1250 B.C.[8] God promised that the Messiah would be prophet like Moses (Deuteronomy 18:15-19).

King David reigned about 1,000 B.C. (1,000 - 960 B.C. to be exact[9]). God promised Jesus would be one of David's descendants (2 Samuel 7:12-16).

---

[7] *Holman Bible Atlas* (Nashville, TN: Broadman & Holman Publishers, 1998), 41-45.

[8] *Holman Bible Atlas*, 63-64.

Jesus was born in either 6 or 4 B.C.[10] He died and rose again in either 30 or 33 A.D.[11] That means these prophecies were written as much as 2,000 years before Jesus was born, lived, and died, fulfilling these and many other prophecies. In fact, Jesus fulfilled at least 353 Old Testament prophecies. The odds of that happening by chance are staggering!

In the book *Science Speaks*, Peter W. Stoner and Robert C. Newman used the science of probability to work out the odds of one person fulfilling just eight of the prophecies about Jesus.

The probability that Jesus would fulfill just eight of these prophecies is one chance in one hundred million billion.[12] That's a one with seventeen zeros after it!

That is a number bigger than I can understand, so let's try to say that in a way easier to picture. The probability scientist Stoner describes it this way. Pretend the entire state of Texas is completely covered with silver dollars stacked two feet deep. It takes *days* to drive across the state of Texas. That's a *lot* of silver dollars!

Now pretend one of those silver dollars has a red X on it. What is the chance that a blindfolded man could start in the middle of Texas, go out in any direction, walking over all those silver dollars, and choose the one with the red X on his very first try?

That sounds impossible, right? That's the probability odds of someone fulfilling just eight prophecies written about the Messiah. Yet Jesus fulfilled at least 353! Only God can do that.

(To study this topic further, I recommend Lee Strobel's *Case for Christ*. It comes in a technical, adult version, a student version, and a children's version.)

Closing Prayer
Lord, You are amazing! Only God could do something as amazing as all that. Thank You for telling us in detail what to expect long before Jesus was born. Please continue to answer our questions and teach us more about You. In Jesus' name we pray, amen.

---

9 *Holman Bible Atlas*, 102.
10 Herod the Great died in 4 B.C. Since he ordered every boy-child killed at was age 2 and younger, one can place the birth of Christ between 6 and 4 B.C.
11 One can arrive at the year of Jesus' death and resurrection by looking for a year in which Passover (Nissan 14 according to the Jewish calendar) was on a Thursday. This places Jesus' death and resurrection in either 30 or 33 A.D.
12 Daryl E. Witmer, "What are the odds surrounding Jesus Christ? Who was this child *really*?" *ChristianAnswers.net*, Website (Marysville, WA: AIIA Institute, 2001), accessed 20 November 2017, https://christiananswers.net/q-aiia/jesus-odds.html; also published in *Areopagus Proclamation*, vol. 4, no. 3; Lee Strobel, *The Case for Christ: A Journalist's Personal Investigation of the Evidence for Jesus* (Grand Rapids, MI: Zondervan, 1998), 183.

Let's play a game. When we talked about the probability that one person would fulfill just eight of the prophecies about Jesus, we compared it to looking for a coin. Let's look for somethings that are a bit easier to find.

Go on an outdoor photo scavenger hunt together. If the weather does not permit, find these items in rooms other than where you've been talking.

Take a picture of a family member with each item. Feel free to add your own items to this list before you begin.

1. Something yellow

2. Something round

3. Something hard

4. Something soft

5. Something square

6. Something red

7. Something that flies

8. Something that shines

9. Something that grows

10. Something that shrinks

11. Something that can be loud

12. Something that loves

13. Something that hurts

14. Something soothing

15. Something refreshing

PRETEEN WEEK 2: PEACE
HOW TO LIVE IN PEACE

Items Needed

For today's lesson, you will need the following:

EITHER

- A tub or baking pan with four sides

- Water

- Items of various sizes to drop in the water

- Plastic table cloth

OR

- A flat tray with four sides (like a cookie sheet)

- Whole milk (low-fat milk will not work for the science experiment)

- Assorted colors of food coloring (at least 3)

- Liquid dish soap

Today's Bible Verses

It may be helpful to look up these verses and bookmark them in advance. Older children and teens can help you.

Don't have a Bible at home? Try http://biblegateway.com. Type the reference below, hit enter, and it will take you right to it.

- Philippians 4:7 (optional - note that we'll be looking at this again later)

- Psalm 139:3-4, 11-12 (optional)

- Isaiah 59:2

- 1 John 1:9

- Romans 10:9-10

- Philippians 1:6 (optional)

- Romans 12 (optional)

- James 5:16

- Philippians 4:4-9

Why are we doing this?

Peace is hard. You're feeling calm and peaceful, then BANG! Someone hurts you, or you run into a tough problem, or someone else's bad attitude rubs off on you. So much for being at peace!

God wants Christians to live at peace with one another, at peace with God, and at peace with ourselves. Sounds impossible, doesn't it? But it's not.

Advent Wreath Candle Guide
Each week, light the previous weeks' candles before moving on to the new one. You may also choose to have the previous weeks' candles already lit and simply light the new one. Once lit, the appropriate candles should burn for the rest of your devotional time. Candles may also be lit at meals or other times.

Today we light two candles: last week's candle of Hope and this week's candle of Peace (both are purple if using a multi-colored set).

Opening Prayer
Lord, please teach us what it means to live at peace. Help us to live at peace with other people, with You, and with ourselves. Teach us to abide in You and in Your peace. In Jesus' name we pray, amen.

What is peace?
We hear a lot about peace at Christmas time, but how often do we actually stop and think about what it means?

What does peace mean? (Let family members answer and give examples.)

Here's a simple definition of peace. Peace is the calm feeling you have inside when you know things are going to be ok.

What is the opposite of peace? (Let family members answer and give examples.)

God gives us perfect peace, even a peace that passes understanding or doesn't make sense (Philippians 4:7). Today we're going to talk about how to get that kind of peace.

Suggested Songs
- "Silent Night"

- "It Came Upon the Midnight Clear"

You have an option here. Choose Activity 1 or Activity 2.

Activity 1: Ripples on the Water

Pour the water into the basin. See how peaceful the water looks?

Take turns dropping various items into the water.

- Do they have a large impact or a small impact?

- How do the ripples from different objects interact with one another?

Activity 2: A Color Symphony

This science experiment is from ScienceBob.com (see link below).

Carefully pour the milk into the tray so that it just covers the bottom. (Low-fat milk will not work for this science experiment.)

Add about 6-8 drops of different colored food coloring onto the milk in different spots. See how peaceful the milk and colors look?

Add about 5 drops of the liquid soap onto the drops of food coloring and watch what happens.

To clean up, simply pour the colored milk down the drain. (Don't drink it!)

(Learn how this works at https://sciencebob.com/a-color-symphony/.)

- What happened?

- Did one reaction impact another? If so, how?

One of the fastest ways to lose peace is to sin. Sometimes when we sin, we think that it doesn't hurt anybody, so it's no big deal. That is not true. Sin always has consequences. Sin breaks our relationship with God and with other people. It may also have natural consequences like the ripples in our experiment. These consequences then affect other people. It is never an isolated event.

Let's look closer at how this works. Pretend an adult asks you if you did your homework. You didn't, but you don't want them to bother you about it. So, you lie and say, "Yes, I did it." The adult may ask, "All of it?" You continue the lie by saying, "Yes." Then the adult leaves you alone. You got what you wanted, right?

Not so fast. The next day, that same adult runs into your teacher at the store. They get to talking about you and it comes out that you didn't do your homework. How do you think the adult might feel when he or she learns that you lied? (Let family members answer.) Do you think that adult will be so quick to take you at your word next time? (Let family members answer.) What other things in your relationship might change? (Let family members answer.)

Let's look at this another way. What if you never get caught? Would there be any consequences if the person you lied to never found out? (Let family members answer.) What things might change in your relationship if they never caught you lying to them? (Let family members answer. Be sure to discuss the possibility of beginning a pattern of lying.)

There's one more thing we need to think about in our lying example. It's not just our relationship with other people that changes when we sin. Our relationship with God also changes. God sees what's in our heart. We cannot hide from Him (Psalm 139:3-4, 11-12). How do you think sin might affect our relationship with God? (Let family members answer.)

If we sin, peace is impossible. Sin, disobedience, and not doing what God asks of us blocks our prayers. It also blocks the work of the Holy Spirit in our lives.

Read Isaiah 59:2.

The first step to peace is to follow the Holy Spirit's leading by believing in Jesus and asking God to forgive us.

Read 1 John 1:9 and Romans 10:9-10.

When we follow the Holy Spirit's leading and ask Jesus to be our Lord and Savior, He wipes away all our sin like it never happened. We may still have to face consequences in our relationships with other people, but God sees us like we never sinned in the first place. I wish I could tell you that from that point on we never sin. That is not the case. God continues to work in our lives, making us more like Jesus as we follow Him, but we will not be perfect until we get to heaven (Philippians 1:6; Romans 12).

We all still mess up and sin. That sin blocks our prayers and stops the work of the Holy Spirit in our lives. The solution is to confess our sin to God and to those we sinned against. Confession is simply telling on yourself, saying you are sorry, and meaning it. In our lying example, you would need to confess to the adult who asked if your homework was finished.

Read James 5:16.

Confession is the first step to peace, but God tells us even more about how to live in His peace. As we read this next set of verses, listen for things we can do to get peace.

Read Philippians 4:4-9.

- What are things we can do to get peace? (Reread the passage as necessary.)

- That stuff isn't always easy. What can you do to remind yourself to do these things?

Take some time to develop a plan of action, asking yourself the following questions:

- When is it hard to remember to do these things?

- What can I do in those moments to remind myself what God says?

- What other things can I change about the way I do certain things that would help me avoid tough situations? (For example, could you pack your backpack after supper so you know you have everything ready for the next day?)

Closing Prayer
Father in heaven, thank You for peace. Peace sounds so good! Please teach us to rest in You so we can live in Your peace. Show us sin in our lives so we can live rightly before You. Show us what we need to change to live in Your peace. Help us to trust You, no matter what. We love You, Lord. In Jesus' name we pray, Amen.

PRETEEN WEEK 3: JOY

THE "GOOD NEWS OF GREAT JOY" ISN'T SOME DUSTY, OLD STORY

Items Needed

For today's activity, we are making a Christmas wreath with a cross on it. You may choose to make a larger one for your family or smaller ones for each person. You will need the following:

- One cross per wreath per wreath (various sizes can be found at craft stores or you can cut them out of yellow construction paper or foam sheet)

- Either (1) an evergreen wreath, (2) cutouts of a wreath on green construction paper, or (3) cutouts of a wreath on green foam sheets [Not feeling artistic? For a simple wreath, cut circles about the size of a bowl. Then cut out a second circle from the middle about the size of a cup. You should be left with a donut shape.)

- Ribbons, stars, and other decorations (stickers work great for cutout wreaths)

- Evergreen sprigs (if using construction paper or foam sheets)

- Glue (Hot glue or crafting wire works best on evergreen wreaths. Glue dots or school glue works best on cutout wreaths.)

- OPTIONAL: the letters J, O, Y

- OPTIONAL: scratch paper and writing utensils

Today's Bible Verses

It may be helpful to look up these verses and bookmark them in advance. Older children and teens can help you.

Don't have a Bible at home? Try http://biblegateway.com. Type the reference below, hit enter, and it will take you right to it.

- Isaiah 9:6-7 (quoted below)

- Luke 2:1-20

- Acts 1:8-11

- 2 Peter 3:8-15 (optional)

This is a longer lesson, so I recommend looking up the following verses in advance or another time. They are referred to in parentheses below.

- Genesis 1-2; 3, especially verse 15; 12:1-9; 18:1-15; 21:1-8; 25:19-26; 32:24-32; 46-47

- Exodus 1:1-7; 3:7-12

- 1 Samuel 13:14

- 2 Samuel 7:8-17

- 2 Kings 17; 24-25

- Matthew 11:4-5

- Hebrews 4:15

- Romans 6:23

- John 3:14-18

- Acts 13:27-33

- 1 Peter 1:3-5

- Romans 10:9-10

- Romans 3:22-24

- Mark 1:1

Why are we doing this?

The story of Christmas can become a boring routine. Every year we read the same thing about the angels and the shepherds. It came become a worn out story and a meaningless ritual. It's just one more thing we *have* to do at Christmas time. It reminds me of an old saying: "Familiarity breads contempt." That just means we can get so used to something that we grow to hate it (or at least wish we didn't have to do it).

Here's the problem with that mindset. This isn't a household chore we're talking about here. The angels called it "good news of great joy" (Luke 2:10). When we approach the narratives of the first Christmas thinking we know it already and we *have* to read it one more time, we miss the point. The reason we read it every Christmas is because it's a *big deal!* This stuff literally changed the world forever. Not only that, this was something people had been anxiously waiting for at least 4,000 years! And you thought waiting for Christmas was bad.

Let's make a deal. At least for our time here together, let's pretend we've never heard what happened that first Christmas. Approach these things with new eyes. Pray and ask God to teach you something new from these familiar events. Put yourself in the story. Pretend you are there with those experiencing these things for the first time. Deal? (Look for everyone's agreement.)

Advent Wreath Candle Guide

Each week, light the previous weeks' candles before moving on to the new one. You may also choose to have the previous weeks' candles already lit and simply light the new one. Once lit, the appropriate candles should burn for the rest of your devotional time. Candles may also be lit at meals or other times.

Today we light the (purple) candle of Hope, the (purple) candle of Peace, and the (PINK) candle of Joy.

Opening Prayer

Dear Lord, thank You for Jesus! Open our hearts and our minds to experience anew the anticipation and announcement of Christ's birth. Don't ever let these narratives become worn out, dusty things we pull out once a year. Teach us to rejoice in You and truly celebrate Christ's birth. In Jesus' name we pray, amen.

Backstory

It's hard to understand why today's lesson is exciting if you don't know what happened before. You see, God's people had been waiting for at least 4,000 years for the good news the angels brought to the shepherds that first Christmas. Before we jump to the climax, let's take a moment to quickly review where we are in human history. As we go through, keep track of the dates. It may be helpful to write them down to keep track. Jesus was born in either 6 or 4 B.C.[13] Think about how long the people in each period of history had to wait before God fulfilled His promise.

God made the world (Genesis 1-2). Humans messed it up by choosing to sin, that is, disobey God (Genesis 3). Humans couldn't fix the sin problem on their own, but God promised that the "seed of the woman," that is one of Eve's descendants, would crush the tempter, Satan (Genesis 3:15).

About 2000 B.C.[14], God called Abraham to leave his home and move to Palestine (Genesis 12:1-9).

- How long was that before Jesus was born?

God promised Abraham that all the families of the earth would be blessed through him (Genesis 12:3). When he was 100 years old, Abraham had a son named Isaac (Genesis 18:1-15; 21:1-8). Isaac then had a son named Jacob (Genesis 25:19-26). God gave Jacob the new name of Israel (Genesis 32:24-32). Jacob, I mean Israel, became the head of the family that would become the nation of Israel (Exodus 1:1-7).

The family of Israel moved to Egypt because of a severe famine in 1750 B.C.[15] (Genesis 46-47).

- How long was that before Jesus was born?

In Egypt, the Israelites were mistreated and served as slaves for 400 years before God sent Moses to bring His people out of Egypt and back into the Promised Land which was Palestine (Exodus 3:7-12).

---

[13] See endnote #2.
[14] *Holeman Bible Atlas*, 45.
[15] *Holeman Bible Atlas*, 49.

When the people finally got there, first judges, then kings ruled the people. They went into battle to protect Israel from the other nations who harassed them. One of the most famous kings of Israel was David who ruled between 1000-960 B.C.[16]

● How long was that before Jesus was born?

David loved God and did his best to live for Him. In fact, David was "a man after God's own heart" (1 Samuel 13:14). God promised David that his family and his kingdom would last forever (2 Samuel 7:8-17). That means that the Savior promised in Genesis 3:15 would be not only a descendant of Eve and Abraham, but also a King from the line of David. Not only that, but this promised King will rule an eternal kingdom, one that will never end.

Unfortunately, the kings and Israelites who lived after David didn't follow God. Because of their sin, God split Israel into two kingdoms--northern Israel and southern Judah (whose rulers followed the line of David). God sent prophets to warn the people to repent of their sin and turn back to God. They didn't listen. So, God sent conquering foreigners to take over the land and send the people into exile (2 Kings 17; 24-25). (Northern Israel fell in 722 B.C.[17] while southern Judah fell in 586 B.C.[18]).

● How long was that before Jesus was born?

The Israelites (also known as Jews) knew this was God's punishment (2 Kings 17:7-23). Some of them followed God, even far from home. Others decided it was easier to do what the people around them were doing. They turned away from God to follow the crowd.

Even in exile, God sent prophets to tell the people to repent of sin and turn back to God. One of the most famous prophets was Isaiah. Some of Isaiah's prophecies told more about the promised Messiah. Here is one of the most well known from Isaiah 9:6-7 (NASB).

"For a child will be born to us, a son will be given to us;
And the government will rest on His shoulders;
And His name will be called Wonderful Counselor, Mighty God,
Eternal Father, Prince of Peace.
[7]There will be no end to the increase of *His* government or of peace,
On the throne of David and over his kingdom,
To establish it and to uphold it with justice and righteousness
From then on and forevermore.
The zeal of the LORD of hosts will accomplish this."

● What do we know about the promised Messiah so far?

---

[16] *Holeman Bible Atlas*, 102.
[17] *Holeman Bible Atlas*, 139, 142.
[18] *Holeman Bible Atlas*, 156.

Isaiah's prophetic ministry lasted from 742 B.C. to at least 701 B.C.[19]

The people got to go back in 539 B.C.[20] to rebuild Jerusalem and the destroyed temple of the Lord (Ezra 1:1-4).

- How long was this before Jesus was born?

Even though the people got to go back home and rebuild, it wasn't the same. The people still longed for the promised Messiah.

Suggested Songs
- "O Come, O Come Emmanuel"
- "Joy to the World"
- "Go Tell It On the Mountain"

Bible Reading
Open your Bible to Luke 2:1-20. As we read today, only the person reading aloud will have their eyes open. Everyone else, close your eyes. Pretend you are experiencing these thing as they happened for the first time. Remember how long the anticipation has been building for this moment. Think about what you see, what you hear, what you smell, and what you feel. Are you ready?

Read Luke 2:1-20.

Tell me what happened. (Allow family members to share and ask questions. Know that if a question stumps you, it's ok to say "I don't know.")

The angels brought "good news of great joy" to the shepherds. Do you remember what it was? (Review Luke 2:10-12 as needed.)

A Savior. This new baby was supposed to be a Savior who is Christ the Lord. A savior is someone who saves someone else. Let's look at how Jesus is our Savior.

If you already know how, this is a good chance for you to remember the amazing things Jesus did for you. Listen and thank God for Jesus. Think about who you could tell about Jesus this Christmas.

---

[19] See endnote #2.
[20] *Holeman Bible Atlas*, 167.

We celebrate Jesus' birth at Christmas, but Jesus didn't stay a baby. He grew to be a child and then an adult. When He was all grown up, Jesus healed the blind, the sick, and people who couldn't walk (Matthew 11:4-5).

Jesus also taught people about sin and God's love. Sin is the wrong choices we make. Sin is anything we think, say, do, or don't do that breaks God's perfect standard. We know that no one is perfect. Romans 3:23 says that everyone has sinned at least once--everyone except Jesus (Hebrews 4:15). Romans 6:23 says that the punishment for sin is death. This is a problem because the death in the Bible can also mean being separated from God and all the good things He is and gives. This is a problem, but God in His love provided the answer (John 3:14-18).

Even though Jesus healed people and did all kinds of good things, not everyone liked Him. Jesus' enemies finally had Him arrested and killed. Jesus died on a cross like the one on our wreaths. That is sad, but here's the "good news of great joy" the angels sang about. When Jesus died, He took the punishment for our sins. And Jesus didn't stay dead! Jesus' friends buried Him in a cave and rolled a big stone over the entrance to seal it. Three days later, Jesus came back to life again! This was proof that God accepted Jesus' payment for our sins (Acts 13:27-33).

Now God offers us a gift better than anything under the tree. If we agree with God that we've messed up and sinned and we believe that Jesus is who He said He was and did what the Bible says He did, then we will be saved. God forgives all of the things we've done wrong and comes to live with us every day of our life. When we die, we'll get to go to heaven to live with God (1 Peter 1:3-5).

Here's the catch. God offers this gift of salvation through Jesus to everybody. But, we have to follow the Holy Spirit's leading and accept that gift before it is ours (Romans 10:9-10). Think of it like a Christmas gift. Let's pretend I made this wreath to give to you. (Hold a wreath in your hand.) Is it yours while I still have it? (Let family members answer. The answer's no.) When is it really yours? (Let family members answer. The answer is when that person takes it.)

God offers us salvation through Jesus Christ. The Holy Spirit works in our hearts, leading us to accept Jesus as our Lord and Savior. We accept that gift by telling God we agree that we've done bad things and are truly sorry for them. We must then believe that Jesus is who the Bible says He is and that He died and came back to life again. Then God forgives us and comes to live with us. Out of our love for God and joy, we then try to live in a way that honors God (Romans 3:22-24; Mark 1:15).

Have you ever done that? (Let family members answer. Help those who desire it to pray, confessing sin and asking Jesus to save them. Don't worry or push if they aren't ready yet. Just give the Holy Spirit more time to work in their hearts as they ask questions and keep learning.)

Think About It
- How would you have felt if you lived in Exile and didn't see any sign of the coming Messiah?

- How would you have felt if you were one of the shepherds the angels visited?

- How would you have felt if you came to the stable and saw a little baby laying in a manger?

- Would you have believed Jesus would grow up to save us from our sins? Why or why not?

The story doesn't end here. Before Jesus ascended into heaven, He gave us a job to do.

Read Acts 1:8-11.

Jesus is coming back someday soon. We don't know exactly when, but we are waiting for God to keep this promise just as God's people waited over 4,000 years for the Messiah. We must be ready when Christ comes again. 1 Thessalonians 5:2 says Jesus will come back like a thief in the night. We won't know when or where.

It'd be like your parents or your pastor suddenly showing up while you were hanging out with your friends or alone in your room. What would they catch you doing? You don't have to answer that, but think for a minute. Jesus could come back anytime. When He does, what will He catch you doing? Will you be living in a way that honors God or not? These are questions that we should take time to seriously think about. It may mean we need to change some things we are doing. Take some time today by yourself to think about these things and decide what in your life needs to change.

OPTIONAL: Read 2 Peter 3:8-15.

Closing Prayer
Thank You God for Jesus. Thank You for the "good news of great joy" that the angels brought to the shepherds. Help us keep looking for You. Give us joy as we remember what Jesus did for us. Give us patience and endurance like the people who followed You, waiting and waiting for the promised Messiah to come. In Christ's name we pray, amen.

Family Fun
People waited a long time for Jesus to come. But, God's people never lost hope because God always keeps His promises. Evergreen leaves (or needles) are always green. Use them to remind you of the long time people waited for Jesus. They didn't give up hope, even though it seemed like it would never happen. When you see other trees changing colors and losing their leaves (even if it's just in pictures), remember the evergreen tree. Remember that God's people never lost hope. As a result, they had great joy when God answered their prayers and gave us a Savior. Praise God for that good news of great joy!

Gather your Christmas wreath supplies and get creative. Make a Christmas wreath you like. Be sure to include a cross.

PRETEEN WEEK 4: LOVE
DIFFERENT KINDS OF LOVE

Items Needed

During today's Family Fun, you will be showing love as a family by offering to help a neighbor or elderly person in your church with yard work or housework. You could also choose to clean your own house, especially if you have company coming for Christmas.

You will need the following:

EITHER

- Yard work tools appropriate for the season (snow shovels, rakes & trash bags, etc.)

- A special snack for when you finish

OR

- Housework tools (vacuum, duster, mop, cleaning supplies, etc.)

- A special snack for when you finish

Today's Bible Verses

It may be helpful to look up these verses and bookmark them in advance. Older children and teens can help you.

Don't have a Bible at home? Try http://biblegateway.com. Type the reference below, hit enter, and it will take you right to it.

- 1 John 4:9-10

- Isaiah 64:6

- Ephesians 2:8-10

- Romans 5:8 (quoted below)

- 1 John 4:11-14

- Micah 6:8 (optional)

- Matthew 25:31-46, especially verses 35-40 (optional)

This is a longer lesson, so I recommend looking up the following verses in advance or another time. They are referred to in parentheses below.

- Genesis 1-3

- 1 Samuel 2:2

- Luke 2

- John 1

- Hebrews 4:15

- Matthew 26:36-28:20

- John 1:12; 3:16

- Romans 6:23; 10:9-10

- Ephesians 2:1-10

Why are we doing this?
We hear the word "love" a lot today. "I love my car." "I love my spouse." "I love my dog." "I love chocolate ice cream." "I love God."

Do we ever stop to think what we really mean by these things? Do we really love God the same way we love our favorite food? Let's take some time to look at what love really means.

Advent Wreath Candle Guide
Each week, light the previous weeks' candles before moving on to the new one. You may also choose to have the previous weeks' candles already lit and simply light the new one. Once lit, the appropriate candles should burn for the rest of your devotional time. Candles may also be lit at meals or other times.

Today we light the (purple) candle of Hope, the (purple) candle of Peace, the (PINK) candle of Joy, and the (purple) candle of Love.

Opening Prayer
Lord, please teach us about love today. Show us how You love. Show us clearly how we love You. Show us how we can love You more. Teach us to share Your love with those around us. In Jesus' name we pray, amen.

Different Kinds of Love
Did you know that the Bible uses more than one word for "love"? The Greeks weren't satisfied with one word conveying the different kinds of love, so different words meant different things. Let's look at a few of these[21] today.

---

[21] For more information, see Roman Krznaric's article "The Ancient Greeks' 6 Words for Love (And Why Knowing Them Can Change Your Life)" published 27 December 2013 with Yes! Magazine, http://www.yesmagazine.org/happiness/the-ancient-greeks-6-words-for-love-and-why-knowing-them-can-change-your-life, accessed 21 November 2017.

One kind of love is purely physical and designed by God to be enjoyed only between a husband and a wife. In Greek it's called *eros* (AIR-oh-s). This is physical love.

A second kind of love is the "good friend" kind of love. In Greek it's called *philos* (fih-lay-oh). The city of Philadelphia, PA, is called the City of Brotherly Love because the name Philadelphia has the word *philos*[22] in it. "Brotherly love" is another way to say it's a "good friend" love.

- Who would you say you *philos* love? (Let family members answer.)

A third kind of love is the "favorite" kind of love. I don't know a Greek word for that, so let's stick with "favorite" love.

- What is one thing that you would say you "favorite" love? (Let family members answer.)

A fourth kind of love is unconditional or "no matter what" love. In Greek it's called *agape* (uh-gah-pay). This love without strings attached is the kind of love God has for us. God is our perfect Father. He shows us how to love other people, especially our families, no matter what.

Let's make sure we understand that right. Not everyone has a good father who tried to love the way God loves. God doesn't love like our earthly parents do. It's supposed to be the other way around. Our earthly fathers and mothers are supposed to follow God's example and love their kids no matter what. Unfortunately, our earthly fathers and mothers aren't perfect and make mistakes. Even though moms and dads mess up from time to time, God shows us what real love looks like as our perfect Father. God is our *perfect* Father. He loves us unconditionally. We can follow His example and love other people the way God loves us.

Suggested Songs
- "Away in a Manger"

- "10,000 Reasons"

- "Love Came Down at Christmas"

Bible Reading
Let's see how God shows His unconditional love for us. Read 1 John 4:9-10.

---

[22] Are you trying to find all of the letters of *phileo* in the name Philadelphia? It doesn't work that way. Philadelphia is a compound word. In Greek that means some letters drop out. "Phil" is all that is left from *philos*. *Adelphos* means "brother," but that ending is also changed slightly in this compound word. Isn't it funny that the name says the same thing twice? It's like the name of the city is actually "brotherly love for my brother" or "good friend love for my brothers and sisters" (the sisters are implied). Pretty cool!

There are some church words in verse 10 that you may not know. Some translations say Jesus was the "atoning sacrifice" while others say He was the "propitiation for our sins." Do you want to guess what that means? (Let family members guess.) To understand what this means, we have to rewind and get some background information.

God made the world and everything in it (Genesis 1-2). God made everything good and perfect like He is perfect (Genesis 1:31; 1 Samuel 2:2).

Since God made everything, He makes the rules. He gave Adam and Eve, the first man and woman, one rule: don't eat from the tree in the middle of the garden where they lived (Genesis 2:16-17). God didn't make people to be robots who had no choice. The love of a robot doesn't mean anything, because they have no choice but to do what they are programed to do. Let's pretend to be robots and say together, "No robot love." Ready? "No robot love." (Repeat if you like.)

God didn't want people's robot love. God wanted people to *choose* to love and obey Him. Unfortunately, Adam and Eve chose to disobey God, break His rule, and sin (Genesis 3:1-6). This broke God's perfect creation. Sin also has consequences. When Adam and Eve chose to sin, death entered the world for the first time (Genesis 3:21, see also verses 19, 22-24; Romans 6:23). They had to leave the beautiful, perfect garden to work hard for their food (Genesis 3:19, 22-24). There were now things that caused humans pain and suffering (Genesis 3:16-19). God's relationship with humans was broken as well as the relationships between people (Genesis 3:16, 22-24).

The world is still broken today. What are some ways you see that the world is broken and no longer perfect? (Let family members answer.)

Sin is anything we think, say, do, or don't do that goes against what God told us to do. Can you name some sins? (Examples may include hitting a sibling or friend, taking a toy that does not belong to you, or lying.)

People try lots of this to try to fix this brokenness. What are some people try to make things better? (Let family members answer. Possible responses include: punishing themselves, trying to be a good person, going to church a lot, following a list of rules, giving money to good causes, doing things for other people, etc.)

Read Isaiah 64:6.

- How does God see our good deeds without Jesus?

- Would it work for me to earn my way to heaven through the things I do or don't do? Why or why not?

The bad news is that the stuff people try to do can't fix our sin problem. Only God can fix it. Read Ephesians 2:8-10.

- Which came first: doing good things or God's saving grace through Jesus Christ?

- Can we do enough good things to balance out the bad and make us right in God's eyes?

Here's the good news. Romans 5:8 says, "But God demonstrates his own love for us in this: While we were still sinners, Christ died for us" (NIV).

That brings us back to "propitiation" or Jesus' "atoning sacrifice for sin." We couldn't fix our sin problem on our own. Only God could do that. So, God sent His Son Jesus to be born as a human baby (John 1; Luke 2). He grew up to be a man and never sinned, not even once! He never sinned in what He thought, what He said, or what He did, and He never didn't do what He was supposed to do (Hebrews 4:15). Jesus lived a perfect life, but some people hated Him. They killed Him by nailing Him to a cross (Matthew 26:36-27:56). When Jesus died, He didn't have to pay for His sins because He didn't have any. Jesus' death payed the penalty for our sins (Romans 5:17).

Are you ready for the best part? Jesus didn't stay dead! His friends buried Him in a cave and sealed Him in. Then, on the third day, Jesus came back to life again (Matthew 27:57-28:20)! Now we have another choice:

1. We can believe that Jesus is who He said He is and did what the Bible says He did.

2. We can keep asking questions to see if it is true.

3. We can say it's not true and we don't believe.

If we *do* believe, we can tell God we're sorry for our sins (and mean it!) and that we believe in Jesus. Then we will be saved and God will forgive all the things we've done wrong (John 1:12; 3:16; Romans 10:9-10).

When we say that Jesus took our punishment for sin so that God can forgive our sins like they never happened, that is "propitiation" or Jesus' "atoning sacrifice for sin." Atoning sacrifice means making the payment so our sins are wiped away like writing erased from a whiteboard. Propitiation means the same thing. Jesus took our punishment so that if we believe in Him and tell God we're truly sorry for our sins, we will be forgiven.

Have you done that? If not, is the Holy Spirit leading you to do that today? What is stopping you from believing in Jesus and repenting of sin? (NOTE: If one of your family members cannot name some sins and/or does not think he or she has ever sinned, do not push them to say the right answers like a robot. They just aren't ready yet to ask Jesus to be their Lord and Savior. Give the Holy Spirit more time to work on their hearts while they keep asking questions.)

God loves us unconditionally, no matter what. That is why He sent Jesus to take our punishment for sin. We love other people and do nice things for them because God loved us first (Ephesians 2:1-10). Read 1 John 4:11-14.

Think About It

People can be nice, do good things, and love other people whether they are Christians or not. The difference is the value of those things in God's eyes.

- How does God see the good things we do if we do not believe in Jesus and live for Him? (Review Isaiah 64:6 if necessary.)

- Why do Christians do these things? (Review 1 John 4:11-14 if necessary.)

- How does God view the good things we do if we do them out of our love for Jesus?

- What are some ways we can show God's love to other people? (Optional: Read Micah 6:8; Matthew 25:31-46, especially verses 35-40.)

Opening Prayer

Lord, thank You for Your love. Thank You for Jesus' sacrifice on our behalf. Please help us to love unconditionally that way You love us. Open our eyes to see opportunities to love and serve others this week. In Jesus' name we pray, amen.

Family Fun

One of the best ways to show love to others is by serving and doing things for them. As a family, visit a neighbor or elderly person in your church and offer to do some yard work or clean their house.

Or you could choose to clean your own house, especially if you have company coming for Christmas. Add interest by assigning tasks not usually given as normal chores.

Make it a game. Here are some suggestions for how. Choose what works best for your family:

- Assign similar tasks to two teams and race. The team that finishes first wins. BUT, the work must be inspected by the judge before a winner is declared. If you cut corners and didn't really finish, your team automatically loses.

- Sing and dance as you work. For example, put two damp cloth rags on the floor, one under each foot. Then twist to the music, scooting across the floor to clean it.

- Use your creativity to create your own game.

After you've finished: Have a special snack and talk about your experience.

- Why did we do all of that today?

- Did the person we helped today earn our love? Why or why not?

- What was your favorite part about today?

- What was your least favorite part about today?

- How did you feel knowing you were showing love and helping out?

- How do you think the neighbor/person from your church/in-coming company felt about what you did?

- How do you think God felt about what we did today?

- What are some other things we can do to show love to others?

PRETEEN CHRISTMAS EVE OR CHRISTMAS DAY: CHRIST WHO WAS JESUS REALLY?

Christmas Alternative

Today's lesson focuses on who Jesus is. If you would rather do this lesson another day and focus on Jesus' birth today, please simply read the following verses together.

Don't have a Bible at home? Try http://biblegateway.com. Type the reference below, hit enter, and it will take you right to it.

- Luke 2:1-21.

- Matthew 2:1-12.

Items Needed

For today's lesson, you will need the following:

- Write the following categories on index cards, scrap paper, or a white board.

    o   Good Man

    o   Wise Teacher

    o   Prophet

    o   Lord

- OPTIONAL: Provide additional writing utensils and index cards/scrap paper/white board space to add the appropriate Scripture references later.

Today's Bible Verses

Here are the verses for today's lesson. It may be helpful to look up these verses and bookmark them in advance. Older children and teens can help you.

Don't have a Bible at home? Try http://biblegateway.com. Type the reference below, hit enter, and it will take you right to it.

- Mark 8:27-28
- Matthew 4:17
- Luke 23:13-15
- Matthew 7:28-29
- John 10:27-30

- John 14:6
- Philippians 2:5-11
- Hebrews 9:14 (optional)
- Luke 18:18-19 (optional)

This is a longer lesson, so I recommend looking up the following verses in advance or another time. They are referred to in parentheses below.

- Acts 1:1-11 (referred to below)
- 2 Timothy 3:16-17 (referred to below)
- 2 Peter 1:16 (referred to below)
- 1 Corinthians 15:3-8 (referred to below)

- Mark 8:29 (quoted below)
- Romans 10:9-10 (referred to below)
- James 1:8 (referred to below)
- John 14:25-26 (referred to below)

Why are we doing this?

If you went out to Walmart and took a survey asking a bunch of different people who Jesus was, you'd get a bunch of different answers. Some people think Jesus was a just a good man or a wise teacher or even a prophet. Some say Jesus is God and should be followed and obeyed as Lord.

"What's the big deal?" some people may ask. "Isn't God the same no matter what you call him?" That sounds good on the surface, but it is a lie. Very few people *like* telling others they are wrong, especially when it comes to big things like what we believe to be true or what happens after we die.

Here's the thing. The truth is the truth no matter what you think about it. Two plus two will always equal four, whether you want it to or not. Something dropped from a height will always be subject to the laws of gravity, whether you want it to or not. The same is true of Jesus. Who He is and what He did stays the same no matter whether you like it or not. That makes it worth investigating who Jesus really is.

Advent Wreath Candle Guide

Each week, light the previous weeks' candles before moving on to the new one. You may also choose to have the previous weeks' candles already lit and simply light the new one. Once lit, the appropriate candles should burn for the rest of your devotional time. Candles may also be lit at meals or other times.

Today we light the four candles from the previous weeks: Hope (purple), Peace (purple), Joy (pink), and Love (purple). Not all advent wreaths have a fifth candle. If you do have a fifth candle, this is the day you light it as well. This is the Christ candle. If your wreath only has four candles, simply light those four.

Opening Prayer
Merry Christmas, Lord! Thank You for Jesus. Thank You for a day to celebrate Christ's birth. This Christmas, please show us more clearly who Jesus really is. In Christ's name we pray, amen.

Eyewitness Testimony
This confusion about Jesus is not new. Even when Jesus lived here on earth people had lots of opinions about who He was.

One of the best ways to figure this out is to look at what Jesus said about Himself.

When Jesus lived on this earth, He asked twelve men to hang out with Him all the time. These men were called the disciples. The disciples followed Jesus around, lived in the same places He did, ate meals with Him, watched what He did, and listened to what He said. During the three years they did this, Jesus taught them many things. Jesus also taught other people who followed Him as much as they could. After Jesus died, came back to life, and ascended into heaven (Acts 1:1-11), Jesus' disciples taught other people about Jesus what Jesus said and did.

God also gave them the words to say to write down what they knew about Jesus (2 Timothy 3:16-17). The Gospels (Matthew, Mark, Luke, and John) are the first four books of the New Testament. They tell us about Jesus' life here on earth. The rest of the New Testament includes references and explanations of what Jesus said and did, but the Gospels simply tell us what happened during Jesus life on earth.

The Gospels were written while people who still knew Jesus were still alive (2 Peter 1:16; 1 Corinthians 15:5-8). That means that if the writer got something wrong, these people would have said something and corrected them. That also means that the writings about Jesus which included made up stuff would not have been included in the Bible. Those who knew better would have made sure the early churches knew they were wrong so that people wouldn't believe a lie. At the end of their lives, the disciples were told they had to either change their stories about Jesus or die. They wouldn't agree, so they died. The disciples died because they knew what they taught about Jesus was true. No one would die trying to protect a lie.

Peter was one of those disciples. He said, "For we did not follow cleverly devised myths when we made known to you the power and coming of our Lord Jesus Christ, but we were eyewitnesses of his majesty" (2 Peter 1:16 ESV).

(To study this topic further, I recommend Lee Strobel's *Case for Christ*. It comes on a technical, adult version, a student version, and a children's version.)

Today we're going to look and see what these eyewitnesses said about Jesus.

Suggested Songs
- "You Shall Call His Name Jesus"

- "What Child Is This"

- "Holy, Holy, Holy"

- "Happy Birthday" to Jesus

Bible Reading

Today's Bible reading is going to be a little different. We're going to match up the Bible verses we read with descriptions of Jesus to see who He really was. (Point out your four categories.)

Lord means that Jesus is the boss. Lord means we should listen to what Jesus says and obey Him.

As we read each verse, tell me where you think it best fits. (Read the following verses one at a time. Some may fit in more than one category.)

- Mark 8:27-28
- John 14:6

- Matthew 4:17
- Philippians 2:5-11

- Luke 23:13-15
- Hebrews 9:14 (optional challenge verse)

- Matthew 7:28-29
- Luke 18:18-19 (optional challenge verse)

- John 10:27-30

Think About It

These are just a few of the things the Bible says about Jesus. Based on these things, was Jesus a good man? (Let family members answer.) Was He only a good man and nothing else? (Let family members answer)

Was Jesus a wise teacher? (Let family members answer.) Was He only a good teacher and nothing else? (Let family members answer.)

Was Jesus a prophet? (Let family members answer.) Was He only a prophet and nothing else? (Let family members answer.)

What does Lord mean again? (Let family members answer. Review as needed.) Is Jesus Lord? (Let family members answer.) Is He only Lord and nothing else? (Let family members answer.)

What else do we know about Jesus? (Let family members answer.)

Jesus once asked His disciples an important question. Mark 8:29 says, "And He continued by questioning them, 'But who do you say that I am?' Peter answered and said to Him, 'You are the Christ'" (NASB). The same question applies to us. Who do you say Jesus is? Don't answer out loud, just think about it.

Who Jesus is doesn't change just because we want it to be different. Still, what we believe about Jesus is very important. Only by believing that Jesus is Lord will we be saved (Romans 10:9-10). It's also ok if you're not sure yet what you think about Jesus. God tells us to keep asking questions and He will continue to show us the answers (James 1:5; John 14:25-26). Let's pray and ask God to do that right now.

Closing Prayer

Thank You, God, for Jesus. Thank You that He did so much for us. Teach us to better understand Jesus as Lord. Continue to teach us more about You and answer our questions. In Jesus' name we pray, amen.

Family Fun

Today we're going to play "Who Am I?" Here's how it works. We'll take turns acting out a certain person. You can say things that person would say and act the way that person would act, but you cannot say the person's name. That is what everyone else is going to try to guess.

(HINT: It may be helpful to narrow down the possibilities by choosing a category like the following: sports figures, movie characters, actors, book characters, Bible people, church leaders.)

When finished playing (or during a break), ask: How do you know who the person is? (Let children answer.) We know Jesus is the Christ, the promised Messiah, because His words and actions have been recorded by people who knew Him during His time here on earth.

Our Christmas Gift to You

ADVENT READINGS FOR YOUR CHURCH

As an additional bonus for buying this eBook, we're including the matching Advent Candle Readings designed for use in worship services.

This book is copyrighted. If you give a copy to a friend without paying for it, that is ***stealing***.

The FREE *Waiting for Christmas: Advent Readings for Corporate Worship* and the complete *Waiting for Christmas: Weekly Family Devotionals for Advent* are available online at http://parentroadmin.com/store-4/.

Email us at info@parentroadmin.com to discuss bulk pricing.

How Does This Work?

In this busy season, it's easy to forget why Christmas is so important. This year, remember God's plan of salvation which began at Creation and is completed in Jesus Christ. As those who came before us looked forward to Jesus' birth at Christmas, let us also look forward to Christ's return this celebration season.

Included below are four Sunday Advent readings and one more for Christmas Eve or Christmas Day. Each reading is between two and three minutes long, if all participants know their lines well.

These readings are designed to be done by families in the corporate worship service. Each family may assign parts as desired, depending on how many people are in the family. Feel free to assign teenagers either the Adult or Child lines.

Which Candle to Light When

An advent wreath is made up of either 4 blue, 4 purple, or 1 pink and 3 purple candles. The four candles are placed evenly in an evergreen wreath surrounding one white candle.

Each week, light the previous weeks' candles before moving on to the new one. You may also choose to have the previous weeks' candles already lit and simply light the new one. Once lit, the appropriate candles should burn for the rest of the service.

The order (going clockwise) should be: Hope (purple, 1st Sunday), Preparation (purple, 2nd Sunday), Joy (pink, 3rd Sunday), Love (purple, 4th Sunday), and the Christ candle (white, Christmas Eve or Day).

Coaching Children

There are several things you can do to help children of any age do well.

1. **Children should memorize all their lines.** It will take some work, but you can do it! That way people can see your face when you talk. Your nose won't be buried behind the paper you are reading and you won't have to worry about the hard to read words.

2. **Record children saying their lines** and play it back to them. Our voices sound funny when we hear a recording, but it helps us know if our words can be understood.

3. **Practice speaking slower and louder** than you normally talk. When we're nervous, we tend to talk faster and softer, so practice speaking slower and louder. You can make this a game (how slow can you go?), but then practice for real by speaking at an understandable slow rate.

4. **Practice in front of different people.** Practice by yourself. Practice with a trusted adult. Practice in front of your toys. Practice in front of your friends.

5. **Before the service, practice where you will actually do this.** Decide who will stand where. Practice with microphones so you can get used to how that sounds (as well as do your sound check). Go through it more than once if you can, including pretending to light the candle.

6. **Pray together before the service.** Ask God to calm any nerves and to help you remember what you are supposed to say when. Ask Him to speak through you. Pray that people in church today would come to know Jesus as their Lord and Savior.

7. **Consider appointing a leader.** The leader's job would be to subtly cue the next person that it is their turn to speak.

Prayer of Dedication

Please bless, O Lord, your daughters, sons,
and the church at large this Christmas season.

May our hearts be turned as we encounter anew
how You came to earth, took our sin upon You.

May those who don't know come to see and hold
You as their Savior and their Lord.

Thank You for hope. Thank You for Light.
For setting our hearts with You now right.

Come quickly, Lord, and set us free.
Make new the world and show Your glory.

Amen

TIPS & TRICKS

- *See "How this Works," "Which Candle to Light When," and "Coaching Children" above.*

- *This script works best memorized because then it seems more like a real conversation. If necessary, you could copy this script and lay it in your Bible to read, but children should have their lines memorized.*

- *It is better if Bible verses are read out of an actual Bible, but the verses are printed out here for your convenience. The exception to this is the first verse a child quotes. John 3:16 should be recited quickly and by memory. It is ok if no one understands what is said for this one verse (see full script below).*

- *You might need to modify the first few lines to fit the way your church does their advent wreath.*

- *When it says, "Light the candle," don't wait for that person to finish lighting the candle before continuing with the script. This might be easier if you work out who will light the candle first. Then assign lines so that person doesn't need to talk again for a little while.*

- *If people laugh, stop and let it get quiet again before you keep going. Otherwise people won't hear what you say.*

Adult: The first candle is the candle of hope. (Light the candle.)

Child: Why do we light special candles before Christmas?

Adult: The four weeks before Christmas are called Advent. Advent is a time of watching and waiting as we look forward to Christmas and Jesus' return.

Child: I know what I'm looking forward to--all the presents!

I want a _________________. *(Fill in a Christmas gift wish. Repeat this line for each child so they can share their Christmas gift wish.)*

Adult: (smile) Yes, we give presents at Christmas, but there is much more to Christmas than that. Do you remember what God gave us at Christmas?

Child: Jesus!

Adult: That's right. We also remember how God's people waited a long time for Jesus, trusting God's promise that one day a Savior would come.

Child: How did they know Jesus was coming?

Adult: Over and over again in the thousands of years before Jesus was born, God told about Him and promised He would come.

For example, Isaiah 9:2 was written 800 years before Jesus was born. It describes Jesus as the King above all kings. Listen.

"The people walking in darkness
have seen a great light;
on those living in the land of deep darkness
a light has dawned" (NIV).

Child: Hey, a light! Just like our candle.

Adult: That's right. Jesus and God's Word help us know God, just like a light helps us see in the darkness.

Isaiah 9:6-7 go on to tell us more about Jesus.

 "For to us a child is born,
to us a son is given,
and the government will be on his shoulders.
And he will be called
Wonderful Counselor, Mighty God,
Everlasting Father, Prince of Peace.
Of the greatness of his government and peace
there will be no end.
He will reign on David's throne
and over his kingdom,
establishing and upholding it
with justice and righteousness
from that time on and forever.
The zeal of the LORD Almighty
will accomplish this" (NIV).

Child: Wow! Jesus sounds important.

Adult: He sure is. Kings are usually the ones in charge. Jesus is in charge of even those great leaders. Jesus is the King of kings. As our king and boss, Jesus deserves our respect. Philippians 2:10 says, "at the name of Jesus every knee should bow, in heaven and on earth and under the earth" (NIV).

Child: Jesus is supposed to be *my* boss and king? I don't know about letting Him take charge. I like being in control. If I let Jesus take charge, would He be a mean king or a nice king?

Adult:	In Matthew 11:29, Jesus says: "Accept my teaching. Learn from me. I am gentle and humble in spirit. And you will be able to get some rest" (ESV). You may not like everything God asks you to do, but we don't have to be discouraged. God knows everything. We do not. God loves us and always has the best for us in mind. We can trust and hope in Jesus because He is always in control, even when life seems to get crazy. Jesus is the King of kings, in charge of everything.

Child:	Praise to the King of kings! Help me to follow you, Jesus. Amen.

TIPS & TRICKS

- *See "How this Works," "Which Candle to Light When," and "Coaching Children" above.*

- *This script works best memorized because then it seems more like a real conversation. If necessary, you could copy this script and lay it in your Bible to read, but children should have their lines memorized.*

- *It is better if Bible verses are read out of an actual Bible, but the verses are printed out here for your convenience. The <u>exception</u> to this is the first verse a child quotes. John 3:16 should be recited quickly and by memory. It is ok if no one understands what is said for this one verse (see full script below).*

- *You might need to modify the first few lines to fit the way your church does their advent wreath.*

- *When it says, "Light the candle," don't wait for that person to finish lighting the candle before continuing with the script. This might be easier if you work out who will light the candle first. Then assign lines so that person doesn't need to talk again for a little while.*

- *If people laugh, stop and let it get quiet again before you keep going. Otherwise people won't hear what you say.*

Child: Last week we lit the candle of hope and learned that Jesus is the King of kings. What is the second candle?

Adult: The second candle is the candle of peace. (Light the candle.)

Do you know what peace is?

Child: Peace is the opposite of war, right? But what does that have to do with Christmas?

Adult: Yes, one definition of peace is the opposite of war, fighting, or trouble. It can also mean being calm or without worry. Do you remember the story of how God led His people out of Egypt, through the wilderness, and into the Promised Land?

Child: Yes. That was with Moses and Joshua, right?

Adult: That's right. That was over a thousand years before Jesus was born. After the people settled in Israel, they forgot to worship and follow God. God would punish them by letting other countries attack and make war.

Child: You punish me when I make bad choices, but it's never with a war.

Adult: That's right. I love you and I want you to learn to make good choices. God loves His people too.
         When the people saw that God was letting this happen, they would turn back to God, telling
         Him they were truly sorry for the times they had done wrong.

Child: You make me say I'm sorry too.

Adult: That's right. It's important to say you are sorry when you mess up. God forgave His people then
         just like He forgives us now because of Jesus Christ. The people worshipped Him for a while
         until they forgot again. This happened over and over again. They were good while David was
         king, but then they forgot and turned away from God with the kings after David. It just got
         worse and worse.

Child: How could it get worse than having God mad at you and being at war?

Adult: The people just didn't understand that only by following God with our whole heart can we have
         peace. Eventually, the Assyrians [*a-sear-ee-ans*] and Babylonians [*bab-ill-own-ee-ans*] came and
         took over. They killed a lot of people, took some to be slaves in a far off country, and destroyed
         homes and cities. Do you think the people felt peace then?

Child: No way! I would have cried if they tore my house down and took me away. What happened
         next?

Adult: God had not given up on His people. Those in foreign countries and those left home could
         remember the promises God gave them before this disaster.

         Isaiah 9:6-7 promised that God would save them, much like He saved them from slavery in
         Egypt. Listen to these words which were written 800 years before Jesus was born.

         "For to us a child is born,
         to us a son is given,
         and the government will be on his shoulders.
         And he will be called
         Wonderful Counselor, Mighty God,
         Everlasting Father, Prince of Peace.
         Of the greatness of his government and peace
         there will be no end.
         He will reign on David's throne
         and over his kingdom,
         establishing and upholding it
         with justice and righteousness
         from that time on and forever.
         The zeal of the LORD Almighty
         will accomplish this" (NIV).

Dear God, please give us peace, even amidst the crazy storms of life. Help us to trust in You. In Jesus' name we pray...

Child: Amen.

TIPS & TRICKS

- *See "How this Works," "Which Candle to Light When," and "Coaching Children" above.*

- *This script works best memorized because then it seems more like a real conversation. If necessary, you could copy this script and lay it in your Bible to read, but children should have their lines memorized.*

- *It is better if Bible verses are read out of an actual Bible, but the verses are printed out here for your convenience. The exception to this is the first verse a child quotes. John 3:16 should be recited quickly and by memory. It is ok if no one understands what is said for this one verse (see full script below).*

- *You might need to modify the first few lines to fit the way your church does their advent wreath.*

- *When it says, "Light the candle," don't wait for that person to finish lighting the candle before continuing with the script. This might be easier if you work out who will light the candle first. Then assign lines so that person doesn't need to talk again for a little while.*

- *If people laugh, stop and let it get quiet again before you keep going. Otherwise people won't hear what you say.*

Adult: The third candle is the candle of joy. (Light the candle.)

Child: Good because last week was sad.

Adult: Luke chapter 2 tells us about when Jesus was born. "And there were shepherds living out in the fields nearby, keeping watch over their flocks at night. An angel of the Lord appeared to them, and the glory of the Lord shone around them, and they were terrified." Do you think the shepherds expected the angels to come that night?

Child: No way!

Adult: The Bible goes on, "But the angel said to them, 'Do not be afraid. I bring you good news that will cause great joy for all the people. Today in the town of David a Savior has been born to you; he is the Messiah, the Lord. This will be a sign to you: You will find a baby wrapped in cloths and lying in a manger.'"

Do you remember what the angels said about the Child before they said where to find Him?

Child: Not really.

Adult: The angels said the Child born was the Savior, Lord, and Messiah.

Child: What does Savior mean?

Adult: Savior means Jesus saves us from our sins. Jesus grew up to die on the cross to take our punishment for sin. If we agree with God that we have sinned and believe in Him, God will take away all of our sins and we can live with Him forever.

Child: What does Lord mean?

Adult: Lord means the one in charge. Jesus is the one in control. He's kind of like our boss. We choose to do what HE says, even when it's hard.

Child: What does Messiah mean?

Adult: Messiah means "Anointed One." That means that Jesus is set apart for something special--to be our Savior and Lord.

God promised a Messiah hundreds of years before Jesus was born. In Habakkuk 2:3, God's people were encouraged to keep looking for the Messiah, even though it looked like God had forgotten to keep His promise:

"For the revelation awaits an appointed time;
it speaks of the end
and will not prove false.
Though it linger, wait for it;
it will certainly come
and will not delay" (NIV).

Child: But God kept His promise and sent a Messiah, didn't He?

Adult: That's right. There were hundreds of prophecies that said what to look for in the coming Messiah. These were written hundreds of years before Jesus was born, but Jesus fulfilled every one. That is a reason to celebrate and praise God!

After telling the shepherds about Jesus, the Bible says, "Suddenly a great company of the heavenly host appeared with the angel, praising God and saying,

'Glory to God in the highest heaven,
and on earth peace to those on whom his favor rests.'

When the angels had left them and gone into heaven, the shepherds said to one another, 'Let's go to Bethlehem and see this thing that has happened, which the Lord has told us about.'"

Child: Yeah, I'd be excited to see that for myself too.

Adult: Just like God's people waited for a Messiah, Savior, and Lord, we now wait for Jesus to keep His promise to come back to earth again. In that day, everyone will see Jesus and worship Him as Lord, but only those who believe in Jesus now will be saved.

Child: You mean Jesus could come back anytime, even today? I'd better go get ready! Maybe I should
         write Him a song like the angels did.

Adult: Good idea! Let's pray.

         Jesus, help us to be ready for Your return. Help us to live for you while we wait.

         Amen.

TIPS & TRICKS

- *See "How this Works," "Which Candle to Light When," and "Coaching Children" above.*

- *This script works best memorized because then it seems more like a real conversation. If necessary, you could copy this script and lay it in your Bible to read, but children should have their lines memorized.*

- *It is better if Bible verses are read out of an actual Bible, but the verses are printed out here for your convenience. The exception to this is the first verse a child quotes. John 3:16 should be recited quickly and by memory. It is ok if no one understands what is said for this one verse (see full script below).*

- *You might need to modify the first few lines to fit the way your church does their advent wreath.*

- *When it says, "Light the candle," don't wait for that person to finish lighting the candle before continuing with the script. This might be easier if you work out who will light the candle first. Then assign lines so that person doesn't need to talk again for a little while.*

- *If people laugh, stop and let it get quiet again before you keep going. Otherwise people won't hear what you say.*

Adult: The fourth candle is the candle of love. (Light the candle.)

Did you know there are different kinds of love?

Child: Really?

Adult: Yes. There is the mushy kind of love like between a husband and wife, the love between a parent and a child, the "you're my friend" kind of love, the love we have for our pets, and the favorite-kind-of-ice-cream love. (*"Ice cream" may be changed to "food" if you prefer.*)

Child: I love _____________! (*Fill in your favorite kind. Repeat this line for each child so they can share what kind they love.*)

Adult: God loves us with a different kind of love. God's love is perfect and unconditional. That means there is nothing we can do to earn God's love or to make Him not love us anymore.

Child: (*Open your eyes wide.*) Really?

Adult: That doesn't mean we should go do a bunch of bad stuff to make God prove it! In fact, the Bible says just that in Romans 6.

The point is that God loves us, no matter what. 1 John 1:7 tells us that love comes from God. It goes on to say in verses 9 and 10:

"Here is how God showed his love among us. He sent his one and only Son into the world. He sent him so we could receive life through him. Here is what love is. It is not that we loved God. It is that he loved us and sent his Son to give his life to pay for our sins" (NIRV).

[*NOTE: If you use a different translation, be sure to explain what the big words mean.*]

Child: So Jesus proved God's love by *dying* for us? Why would someone die to prove their love?

Adult: Jesus said in John 14:13-14, "Greater love has no one than this: to lay down one's life for one's friends. You are my friends if you do what I command" (NIV).

Child: Wait a minute. Jesus died because of me?

Adult: When Jesus grew up, He lived a perfect life and then died to take your punishment for sin and mine. But He didn't stay dead. After three days in a sealed up tomb, Jesus came back to life again! He ate with His friends and showed Himself to over 500 people before He went up into heaven. He is still alive there today, sitting at the right hand of God.

Child: Wow! Jesus must love us a *whole lot*.

Adult: Yes, He does. In John 14:9-14 Jesus says, "Just as the Father has loved me, I have loved you. Now remain in my love. If you obey my commands, you will remain in my love. In the same way, I have obeyed my Father's commands and remain in his love. I have told you this so that you will have the same joy that I have. I also want your joy to be complete. Here is my command. Love one another, just as I have loved you" (NIRV).

Child: So Jesus died for us and came back to life again because He loves us.

Adult: Yes.

Child: And all He wants in return is for me to love other people?

Adult: That's part of it. Jesus also said to obey His commandments. One of those commandments is to tell God we're truly sorry for our sins and trust Jesus as our Savior and Lord.

Child: That means we ask Jesus to save us from our sin and make Him our boss, right?

Adult: That's right. John 1:12 says, "Yet to all who did receive him, to those who believed in his name, he gave the right to become children of God" (NIV).

As part of God's family, we show our love for God the Father by obeying Him and loving other people.

Child: But what if God asks me to do something that would be mean or hurt someone else?

Adult: God's love is perfect love. Sometimes perfect love shows us where we've messed up, but it always shows us how to turn back and be in a good relationship with God once more. Keep reading your Bible. God will show you how to love other people the way God loves us.

Child: Ok.

Adult: Dear God, thank You for sending Jesus at Christmas to show us Your love. Please remind us how much You love us. Teach us to love other people the way You love. In Jesus' name we pray...

Child: Amen.

TIPS & TRICKS

- *See "How this Works," "Which Candle to Light When," and "Coaching Children" above.*

- *This script works best memorized because then it seems more like a real conversation. If necessary, you could copy this script and lay it in your Bible to read, but children should have their lines memorized.*

- *It is better if Bible verses are read out of an actual Bible, but the verses are printed out here for your convenience. The <u>exception</u> to this is the first verse a child quotes. John 3:16 should be recited quickly and by memory. It is ok if no one understands what is said for this one verse (see full script below).*

- *You might need to modify the first few lines to fit the way your church does their advent wreath.*

- *When it says, "Light the candle," don't wait for that person to finish lighting the candle before continuing with the script. This might be easier if you work out who will light the candle first. Then assign lines so that person doesn't need to talk again for a little while.*

- *If people laugh, stop and let it get quiet again before you keep going. Otherwise people won't hear what you say.*

Child: It's Christmas! It's Christmas! It's finally Christmas!

Adult: I know! Isn't it exciting?

Child: Do we finally get to light the special candle?

Adult: Yes, we do. The candle in the middle is called the Christ candle. (Light the candle.)

Child: Christ. Isn't that another name for Jesus?

Adult: Yes it is. Christmas is all about Christ, that is Jesus.

Child: (sheepishly) And I thought it was all about presents.

Adult: What have you learned this year in our time waiting for Christmas?

Child: I learned that Christmas is really about Jesus.

   God promised Jesus would come a long time before He was born.

   Jesus is the King. He's in charge of everyone and everything.

   And He's coming back again soon!

God has punishments for our bad choices, but He loves us too.

God proved how much He loves us by sending Jesus to take the punishment we deserve.

That shows us that He loves us a lot!

And we're supposed to love each other because of God loves us.

That way people can see God working through us.

Adult: Wow! You've really be listening. I'm proud of you.

Jesus isn't just God's Son. He's also God Himself, but in a human body. You see, God is so big and powerful and holy that humans who look at Him would die. Moses got a glimpse of God's glory in Exodus 33:18-34:8 and Isaiah saw the robe of God filling the temple in heaven in Isaiah 6. Both men immediately fell down and worshipped God. And they didn't even see God's face!

Child: God sounds scary.

Adult: God is perfect and holy while we are not. That makes it impossible for sinful people like you and me to just come into His presence like it's no big deal. But God loves us and wanted to make a way for us to come to Him. That is why He sent Jesus. Jesus is God in a human body. He is a way for people to see God, to touch Him, and to better understand Him. Look at what it says about Jesus in John 1:14. "The Word became a human being. He made his home with us. We have seen his glory. It is the glory of the One and Only, who came from the Father. And the Word was full of grace and truth" (NIRV).

Child: I don't understand.

Adult: All of that amazing glory of God that Moses and Isaiah caught a glimpse of was wrapped up in Jesus. Philippians 2:5-11 explains Jesus this way.

"Who, being in very nature God,
did not consider equality with God something to be used to his own advantage;
7rather, he made himself nothing
by taking the very nature of a servant,
being made in human likeness.
8And being found in appearance as a man,
he humbled himself
by becoming obedient to death--
even death on a cross!

9Therefore God exalted him to the highest place
and gave him the name that is above every name,
10that at the name of Jesus every knee should bow,
in heaven and on earth and under the earth,

[11]and every tongue acknowledge that Jesus Christ is Lord,
to the glory of God the Father" (NIV).

God loves us so much that He sent Jesus to become a human, to live a perfect life, and to take our punishment for sin. He did this so that "whoever believes in Him will not perish but will have eternal life."

Child: Just like it says in John 3:16!

Adult: That's right. We can come and be in the presence of our Holy God because of what Jesus did on the cross.

Jesus, thank You for being born at Christmas. Thank You for growing up and dying for our sins, and then coming back to life again. Thank You for helping us better understand God. Teach us more about You today. In Jesus' name we pray...

Child: Amen.

About the Author

Nancy Ruth has been serving in children's ministry since the seventh grade. She's served on staff and as a volunteer at churches in four states and three denominations. She holds a Master of Divinity and is currently working on a Master of Christian Service in Apologetics. Nancy lives in a hundred year old house that has been in the family four generations. She's looking forward to the candlelight Christmas Eve service and celebrating with a full house of family once again this Christmas.

Learn more about Nancy Ruth and Parent Road Ministries at parentroadmin.com.

Made in the USA
Middletown, DE
24 November 2024

65334033R00071